# Unleashing the Startup Unicorn

# Unleashing the Startup Unicorn

*Breaking Through Constraints to the Entrepreneurial Spirit*

Vivek Kale

**BEP**

BUSINESS EXPERT PRESS

*Leader in applied, concise business books*

*Unleashing the Startup Unicorn: Breaking Through Constraints to the Entrepreneurial Spirit*

Copyright © Business Expert Press, LLC, 2024

Cover design by Charlene Kronstedt

Interior design by Exeter Premedia Services Private Ltd., Chennai, India

First published in 2024 by
Business Expert Press, LLC
222 East 46th Street, New York, NY 10017
www.businessexpertpress.com

ISBN-13: 978-1-63742-563-3 (paperback)
ISBN-13: 978-1-63742-564-0 (e-book)

Business Expert Press Entrepreneurship and Small Business Management Collection

First edition: 2024

10 9 8 7 6 5 4 3 2 1

*To*
*My grandson Anay*
*Anay la pahun samajta manushya janma la vardan ka mhanatat.*

# Description

For a high-tech startup, usually there is no shortage of advice available to help them, but too often the individual subjects are treated in isolation without a means of drawing the whole picture together from the point of view of all stakeholders—especially the investors. This book attempts to fill that gap.

It is well known that high-tech startups need to innovate to survive, yet the failure rate for innovation is shockingly high. Nearly three out of four new products or services, that is, their startups miss their revenue and profit goals—or fail entirely. It is a misconception that high-tech startups fail only because of the failing products or finances—the failures could also be because of erroneous choice of technology platforms, development teams or methodology or even the project execution. Accordingly, this book takes a holistic view of a startup's aesthetics that enables it to become attractive to all stakeholders especially investors in all aspects of its operations at all stages of its lifecycle (seed, first, second, and third round funding and so on till attaining unicorn status or exit).

Above all, the shockingly low number of unicorns per year (i.e., startups whose valuation exceed U.S.$ 1 billion within a timeframe of three to five years)—which is typically less than 0.001 percent—underlines the significance of all and sundry factors contributing to the outstanding success of the venture. In light of these numbers, it can be safely assumed that even veterans in the startup industry may not have lived through the lifecycle of more than a couple of successful startups. The reality of the exceedingly low number of unicorns emerging worldwide every year suggests two main consequences. First, most of the critical aspects of a unicorn are not really enabling imperatives but more in the nature of operational and organizational constraints imposed on the entrepreneurial spirit of the unicorn. Spread across the whole of the book are several examples of such constraints like ambidextrous innovative entrepreneurship, network organization, management by teams, talent management, role-based rather than function-based responsibilities and so on. Second, since no two unicorns are ever similar in any way, the limited range of time period implies that in the absence of prior relevant anecdotal or referential experiences or best practices directly applicable to the critical factors or dimensions of a startup's organization or operations in the real world, adoption of a preconceived theoretical (and untested) contextual framework is inevitable—which is also reflected in the approach of this book. No amount of case studies can truly fulfil these inevitable gaps that have to be confronted by every unicorn afresh.

To succinctly cover all aspects of a contemporary startup, this book has been organized to reflect the natural grouping of competencies that are essential for entrepreneurial ventures, from conception to attainment of unicorn status or successful exit. To understand and analyze these competencies, the book uses an extended 9S model inspired by the pioneering McKinsey 7S model.

# Keywords

startup; unicorn; confluence of exponentials; exponential technologies; McKinsey 7S model; extended 9S model; venture capital; valuation; term sheet; capitalization tables; customer centricity; mass innovation; cognitive advantage; built_to_innovate organizations; intellectual capital; innovative entrepreneurship; ambidexterity; continuous innovation; business model; learning organizations; experimental software development; multiparadigm development; nature-inspired strategies and solutions; bias; safety; offerings of products, services and experiences; TRIZ; network businesses; network of projects; management by teams; talent management; employee engagement; narrow; general and super AI; chatbots; OpenAI GPT-3; modeling and simulations (M&S); digital twins; design thinking; DevSecOps; networks; sensors; platforms; internet of things (IoT), ecosystems bio; nano and industry 4.0; governance; decentralized accounting; decentralized finance (DeFi); security; privacy; trust; blockchain

# Contents

# Preface

This book has been written as a guide for entrepreneurial businesses. A startup's aesthetics in terms of investor's view encompasses the business idea, business model, business execution, and delivery of products/services/experiences to the target segment of customers. It looks at aspects of venture capital (VC) financing and what investors look for in a startup.

The challenge for many entrepreneurs is that they are not familiar enough with issues of finance, management or even technology to recognize what questions they need to ask and answer in order to fill in the gaps. Once they pose such questions to themselves, they are in a position to take full advantage of their keen logic and intellect and direct most of their passionate energies to the business aspects of their venture.

The shockingly low number of unicorns per year (i.e., startups that exceed valuation of U.S.$1 billion—which is typically less than 0.001 percent—underline the significance of *all and sundry* factors contributing to the outstanding success of the venture. The extended 9S model provides a practical and integrated framework that obviates the possibility of the entrepreneur being overwhelmed or benumbed by attending to the myriad of details related to the management and operations of their entrepreneurial venture.

No other book examines the issues specific to high-tech entrepreneurs in a comprehensive manner. Indeed, entrepreneurs would be wise to consider this book as a primer before reading books that examine more specific areas, such as VC, writing a business plan, negotiating term sheets, or on appropriate technologies and methodologies. Reading this book first should enable entrepreneurs to more effectively comprehend, synthesize, and place in proper perspective the information in these follow-up books. The purpose of the book is not to provide all the answers or a blueprint for success of a specific startup; rather, its aim is to stimulate readers to think in strategic terms.

# How Is the Book Different?

This book is unique in several ways. This book takes a holistic view of a startup's aesthetics that enables it to be attractive for all stakeholders, especially investors in all aspects of its operations at all stages of its lifecycle (seed, first, second, and third round funding, and so on till attaining unicorn or exit). A contemporary startup's aesthetics, in terms of the investor's view, encompasses the business idea, business model, business execution, and delivery of products/services/experiences to the target segment of customers. This book covers all of these characteristics aspects across its 12 chapters.

On perusing the table of contents (TOC), it may seem a whole lot of concepts and tools for entrepreneurs to keep track of while running 100 miles an hour trying to launch and run their startup, but all of this is very relevant to a startup that is typically enamored by its own technology, but unaware and unencumbered by other critical success factors. While the relative weights that can be attributed to the various factors in particular circumstances is debatable, this book presents the best choice options of strategies or approaches for various startup imperatives identified in the book.

Here are the characteristic features of this book:

1. It looks at aspects of VC financing and what investors look for in a contemporary startup, for example, exponential growth potential and its realization.

2. It describes the extended 9S model essential for covering all aspects of entrepreneurial ventures, namely, shared values, strategy, structure, stuff, style, staff, skills, systems, and security.

3. It shows how only an overarching aspiration for a startup to become a unicorn is sufficient to explain the typical characteristics of legendry Silicon Valley unicorns like Google, Facebook, LinkedIn, and Twitter.

4. It highlights natural constraints on the entrepreneurial spirit of the exponentially aspiring unicorn, namely, ambidextrous innovative

entrepreneurship, network organization, management by teams, not human resources but talent management, role-based rather than function-based responsibilities, employee engagement, and so on.

5. It describes the approach of design thinking essential for generating creative solutions as also the project management methodology for sharper execution of the high-tech engineering projects.

6. It covers major application areas of current/future interest, namely, intelligent systems (AI/ML/DL), intelligent assistants, wireless sensor networks, Internet of Things (IoT) as also Industry 4.0 (termed as Industrial IoT in the United States) applications, and, blockchain systems.

7. It reveals the contemporary skillsets in demand for startups: design thinking, data science, Generative AI like OpenAI GPT-3, machine learning (ML), deep learning (DL), and Development Security Operations (DevSecOps).

8. It is not focused on any particular technology, or commercial product, platform, or service offering.

## How Is the Book Organized?

This book has been organized to reflect the natural grouping of competencies that are essential for entrepreneurial ventures, from conception to successful exit. To understand and analyze these competencies, the book uses the extended 9S model, namely, shared values, strategy, structure, stuff, style, staff, skills, systems, and security.

Chapter 1 sets the context for the whole book, with its focus on the rationale for the search for exponentials—the benchmark for which was set by the Moore's law powering the growth during the Third Industrial Revolution (1969–2000). The mantle for powering the Fourth Industrial Revolution in the 21st century falls on the class of intelligent systems, including artificial intelligence (AI), machine intelligence (ML), and deep learning (DL). The latter half of the chapter presents unicorns as the engines of growth for the 21st century.

Chapter 2 describes the startup lifecycle and associated aspects related to VC financing. It explains the investment models and priorities as also the startup valuation and related capitalization tables. It explains how the VC's investment model typically renders unicorn aspirations for startups inevitable.

Chapter 3 sets the operative framework for the remaining part of the book. It describes the extended 9S model framework for business excellence—consisting of shared values, strategy, style, stuff, structure, staff, skills, systems, and security. It explains the distinction between (say) shared values and style or strategy and structure, which seem to have overlapping aspects that are sometimes confusing.

Chapter 4 discusses the shared values that are vital for the success of contemporary startups, namely, customer centricity, mass innovation, cognitive advantage, generalized sustainability, increasing complexity of enterprises, and offerings. It introduces mass innovation as the next level of customer centricity as well as the drive for cognitive advantage that underlies the current overwhelming demand for intelligent systems.

Chapter 5 presents aspects related to strategizing for the success of the contemporary digital enterprises, including intangible capital, intellectual capital, ambidexterity, scaling, entrepreneurship, business model, and growth. It highlights aspects related to unleashing the unicorn, namely, Built_to_Innovate organization, scaling, continuous innovation, and growth.

Chapter 6 presents an overview of contemporary software development efforts characterized by customer empathy, experiments and iterations, multiparadigm, multisite, and multiorganization development, and focus on domain-specific functionalities. It introduces the current trend of utilizing nature-inspired strategies and solutions for rapid computations and validations.

Chapter 7 presents an overview of the products, services, and experiences forming the core offerings provided by the startup. While introducing augmented reality (AR) and virtual reality (VR) solutions, it highlights that products can be mass produced for customers. Services can be mass customized for customer preferences and experiences can be mass innovated for customer preferences.

Chapter 8 presents aspects of organizational structures that are most conducive for periods of diverse, high-intensity resources, and efforts, and when required, also of explosive growth. It gives an overview of the efficacy of network structures as embodied in real-life *network of projects,* including with partners and alliances.

Chapter 9 presents aspects of building high-performance teams, including team-based management, not human resources but talent management, role-based rather than function-based responsibilities, employee engagement, team building, personnel and team performance management, and so on. This chapter highlights a factor that is very critical for a startup: long-run consistent productive results are always delivered by the *optimal* effort of a team and not by a team of *superhuman* individuals. Also, a team working together can overcome all possible encountered problems easily—there is no need for every member to have every useful ability or skill.

Chapter 10 presents skills essential for productive teams of entrepreneurial ventures in the 21st century, namely, data science, intelligent systems development (narrow, general and super AI), and design thinking. It introduces digital twins as the next level of approach to modelling and simulation.

Chapter 11 presents details on currently available foundational systems like sensor networks, Internet of Things (IoT), and Industry 4.0 (also termed as Industrial IoT (IIoT) in the United States) that are essential for any startup of the 21st century. It highlights how the transition from internally focused to network-, platform-, and ecosystem-centric ways of working brings with it many practical advantages. It allows for companies to focus on their core competencies and to progressively outsource all activities that are not strategic to the company.

Chapter 12 describes critical issues of governance, identity, trust, privacy, and security. It then introduces blockchain as the panacea for addressing all these constellation of requirements. It highlights how the decentralized aspects of blockchain give rise to unique solutions like triple-entry accounting (TEA) and decentralized finance (DeFi).

Please note that the figures, tables, and references are cited across the whole text as also the Appendix which is accessible online by using this path www.businessexpresspress/.

## Who Should Read This Book?

This book will be of interest to:

- Venture capitalists (VCs), angel investors, and investment managers
- Startup founding leaders

- Business analysts, enterprise architects, and solution architects
- Functional and technical members
- Technology and project managers
- Developers and team members
- Technical managers, business experts and professionals interested in startups and unicorns
- Students of engineering, management, computer, and technology courses interested in startups and unicorns
- General readers interested in the phenomenon of startups and unicorn

Vivek Kale
Mumbai, India.

# Acknowledgments

I would like to thank all those who have helped me with their clarifications, criticism, and valuable information during the writing of this book.

Thanks to Scott Isenberg for making this book happen and guiding it through to completion.

I thank our beloved daughters Tanaya and Atmaja for their understanding and support. And finally, to my wife, Girija, I am grateful, beyond measure, for her continuous loving support and help.

Vivek Kale
Mumbai, India

# Prologue

This book shows how setting an overarching aspiration for a startup to become a unicorn is sufficient to dictate the essential nature of characteristics along the select dimensions of:

*Shared values*: customer centricity, mass innovation, cognitive advantage

*Strategy*: Build_to_Innovate Organization, intangible capital, scaling Continuous innovation, business model, growth strategy

*Style*: Experimental software development, naultiparadigm development, nature-inspired and strategies, bias, safety

*Stuff*: Products, services, experiences, augmented reality (AR), and virtual reality (VR), TRIZ

*Structure*: Network organization model, virtual organization, collaboration networks, networks of projects

*Staff*: Team-based management, Not human resources but talent Management, employee engagement

*Skills*: Data science, intelligent systems (AI, ML, DL, generative AI), modeling and simulation, development security operations (DevSecOps)

*Systems*: Network systems, platform systems (IoT), ecosystems (bio, nano, Industry 4.0)

*Security*: Governance, identity, trust, privacy, security, blockchain

It should not be a surprise if these characteristics seem to match the characteristics of top successful Silicon Valley startups like Google, Facebook, LinkedIn, and Twitter—they all have been legendry pioneering unicorns of their times.

After reading the book, if the reader concludes that the preceding characteristics are the most natural choice options for each of the mentioned characteristics for a contemporary unicorn, then it would have achieved its objective.

# CHAPTER 1

# In Search of Exponentials

## Topics Covered

- Industrial Revolutions at a Glance
- Moore's Law Powering the Third Industrial Revolution
- Exponential Technologies
  ○ Artificial Intelligence as an Exponential Technology
- Startup as a fount of Unicorn
- Genesis of a Startup
- Unicorns as Confluence of Exponentials
  ○ India Startup Ecosystem
- Innovation Gap in Life Sciences
  ○ Blockbuster Drugs
- Unicorns as Engines of Growth in the 21st Century

## Introduction

*This chapter sets the context for the whole book, with its focus on the rationale for the search for exponentials—the benchmark for which was set and by the Moore's law powering the growth during the Third Industrial Revolution (1969–2000). It highlights how the Third Industrial Revolution in the 20th century was powered by Moore's law and industrial clusters were the growth engines of the world economy in the 20th century. It proposes that the Fourth Industrial Revolution in the 21st century will be powered by Artificial Intelligence (AI) systems, and unicorns employing AI systems would be the growth engines of the world economy for the 21st century. Hence, the search for the exponential unicorns.*

## Industrial Revolutions at a Glance

Evolution refers to change that happens gradually as a process. When an analog dialup phone changes to a digital-up phone, it is an evolutionary change from one phase to another phase. On the other hand, when these phones change mobile/smart phones, the change is radical and affects the fundamentals of phone technologies. In that sense, mobile phone technology can be labeled as a revolution.

Industrial revolutions highlighted patterns of exponential growth that were unprecedented.

An overview of the four industrial revolutions is available in the Appendix section (**A1.1 Industrial Revolutions at a Glance**) available online.

## Moore's Law Powering the Third Industrial Revolution

The Third Industrial Revolution was characterized by an exponential decrease—primarily associated with the periodically halving of costs of transistors that underlay more than half a millennium of exponential growth in the IT industry and, consequently, the global economy. On April 19, 1965, Gordon Moore, the cofounder of Intel Corporation, published an article in *Electronics Magazine* entitled *Cramming More Components onto Integrated Circuits* in which he identified and conjectured a trend that computing power would double every two years. This was termed as Moore's law in 1970 by the CalTech professor and VLSI pioneer, Calvin Mead. This law has been able to predict reliably both the reduction in costs and the improvements in computing capability of microchips, and those predictions have held true for more than 50 years (Lambrechts et al. 2019; Tigelaar 2020). Moore's law is not only an expression of a powerful engine for economic growth in the industry but also for the economy as a whole.

Theoretically, Moore's law will run out of steam somewhere in the not-too-distant a future. The possible reasons are:

- The ability of a microprocessor silicon-etched track or circuit to carry an electrical charge has a theoretical limit. At some point when these circuits get physically too small and can no longer carry a charge or the electrical charge bleeds, then we will have a design limitation problem.

- The relentless increase in the manufacturing costs with each successive generation of chip technology. In fact, Gordon Moore had said that, as tolerances become tighter, each new generation of chips requires a doubling in cost of the manufacturing facility. At some point, it will theoretically become too costly to develop the manufacturing plants that produce these chips. The usable limit for semiconductor process technology will be reached when chip process geometries shrink to be smaller than 20 nanometers (nm) to 18 nm nodes. At those nodes, the industry will start getting to the point where semiconductor manufacturing tools are too expensive to depreciate with volume production, that is, their costs will be so high that the value of their lifetime productivity can never justify it.

- The power requirements of chips are also increasing. More power being equivalent to more heat equivalent to bigger batteries implies that at some point, it becomes increasingly difficult to power these chips while putting them on smaller platforms.

Each of the industry revolutions was associated with a characteristic exponential phenomenon that powered growth during that period. Even the auto industry had shown similar declines in costs during its initial period. At the turn of the 20th century, cars were luxury items, which typically sold for U.S.$20,000. Henry Ford revolutionized the auto industry with the invention of the assembly line. Ford's efforts resulted in a steady reduction in costs, quickly bringing the cost of manufacturing a car to under U.S.$1,000. But, even Ford's ability to reduce costs had bottomed out by 1918.

At the beginning of 20th century, rapid advances in agricultural techniques instead of slowing economic growth, buoyed it as they freed up human resources to work on other things, which in turn made possible the industrial age in the latter part of the millennium. Mechanized transportation allowed centralized manufacturing, so factories could achieve greater economies of scale. This combined with the mechanization of the factory greatly enabled improved productivity, thus resulting in greater noninflationary growth levels. As industry grew to be a larger part of the economy, it pushed economic growth up to an average of about 3 percent, instead of slowing it down to the 1 percent annual economic growth of agricultural economies. Since the latter half of the 1990s, the United States has been able to achieve regular noninflationary growth of 4 to 5 percent because of productivity gains made possible by IT industry.

In the case of semiconductors, where the gains have been made, have largely been on account of lithography. As long as Moore's law brought us exponential progress in hardware through apparently incessant scaling of the devices (in terms of density, i.e., number of transistors per square area), progress in performance was always assured and progress in architecture, and software could be viewed as an additional side benefit. But as we begin approaching closer to the end of scaling, all there is left to progress is enterprise architecture and software applications like AI and ML (see *Artificial Intelligence as an Exponential Technology* subsection and Chapter 10, *Skills*).

## Exponential Technologies

In 2005, the inventor and futurist Ray Kurzweil published the book *The Singularity Is Near: When Humans Transcend Biology* where he describes the law of accelerating returns, which predicts an exponential increase in the capacity of technologies like computers, genetics, nanotechnology, robotics, and AI. This increase is driven by a technological discontinuity or inflection point, or singularity is able to redefine the ways entire markets and industries operate. The impact of such disruptive change is not limited to industries and organizations but rather pervasive on the life of individuals, societies, and nations as a whole.

The emergence of a digital economy determines a new industrial system Industry 4.0, grounded on the use of Internet of Things (IoT) and cyberphysical systems (CPS) to analyze, automate, and monitor the business operations. The combination of these forces contributes to create a new pattern for developing societies and business organizations. In particular, the disruptive cumulative effects from the deployment of complex interrelated technology systems can drive a transition from a linear to exponential or a more complex model of operational efficiency and economic evolution (Espindola and Wright 2021; Calvo 2020). Such transition is able to generate huge opportunities for organizations to create economic and social value. In particular, leading organizations are those aiming to expand their boundaries to embrace open innovation and are able to continuously stimulate the corporate innovation process.

The exponential growth mechanisms of the new technologies and their impact on business development and societal wealth creation have been explicated by Ismail (2014) using a model of six $D$, namely:

    i. Digitization of products, services, and processes means that they can be replicated and sold for close to zero marginal cost, for example, searching for best-match products.

    ii. Deceptive as the incremental growth seems small at first while the technology is in its infancy, for example, digital cameras.

    iii. Disruptive because the initial growth of a small technology can result in massive, disruptive growth.

    iv. Dematerialization as products, services, and processes can be made available (almost) for free, for example, in the form of apps, GPS, high-resolution cameras, online books, podcasts, and so on.

    v. Demonetization as the cost for a digitized technology drops significantly and extends use, for example, digital photography.

    vi. Democratization as the products and services powered by this technology can become available for everyone in principle connecting all people on the planet.

### AI as an Exponential Technology

Much of the contemporary excitement around AI flows from the promise of a particular set of techniques known collectively as ML. ML refers to the capacity of a system to learn and improve its performance at a task over time involving recognizing patterns in datasets. Another AI technique that is increasingly seen as being behind recent advancements is deep learning (DL), which leverages many layered structures to extract features from enormous datasets (see Chapter 10, *Skills*).

It is important to highlight that this book does not discuss other promising potentially exponential technologies like big data, analytics, cloud computing, mobile computing, and so on. This is not in any way indicative of their lesser significance. On the contrary, they are important prerequisites for all the concepts, technologies, and aspects discussed in this book. Notwithstanding their promise as exponential technologies, they do not rate very high when compared with the potential *cognitive advantage* of the elk of AI (and ML and DL) based intelligent systems (see Chapter 4, *Cognitive Advantage* subsection).

In light of the strides made in the area of chatbots with products like OpenAI's GPT-3, it is evident that AI/ML/DL has the best potential to shoulder the responsibility to continue the progress of Moore's law, albeit for an enlarged time cycle of (say) 2.5 years.

## Risk of Extinction From AI

In a letter published by the nonprofit Center for AI Safety (CAIS) in June 1923, more than 350 signatories stated that mitigating the risk of extinction from AI should be a global priority alongside other societal-scale risks such as pandemic and nuclear war. Among them were two of the so-called *godfathers of AI* who received the 2018 Turing Award for their work on DL, namely, Geoffrey Hinton and Yoshua Benglo, and professors from institutes ranging from Harvard to China's Tsinghua University. The third godfather of AI, Yann LeCun, working at Meta, did not sign the letter.

Recent developments in AI have sparked fears that the technology could lead to privacy violations, powerful misinformation campaigns, and lead to issues with *smart machines* thinking for themselves. AI pioneer Geoffrey Hinton had stated earlier that that AI could pose a more urgent threat to humanity than climate change. Recent advancements in large language models (LLMs)—the type of AI systems used by ChatGPT and other chatbots—have raised fears that AI could soon be used at scale to spread misinformation and propaganda, or that it could eliminate millions of white-collar jobs. In May 2023, Sam Altman, CEO of OpenAI, called on American lawmakers to regulate AI in a 2.5-hour long testimony in the U.S. Congress.

Additional details are available in the Appendix section (**A.1.2 Artificial Intelligence as an Exponential Technology**) available online.

## Startup as the Fount of Unicorn

The age of exponential technology is rapidly becoming a reality to generate business excellence and social progress for the future. This will require a new approach to technological discovery and innovation in organizations and societies that holds the potential to connect and exploit the collective intelligence of many engaged individuals to develop new entrepreneurial business ventures. It will also require a new breed of exponential-driven organizations like unicorns with appropriate leadership approaches and management skills to succeed.

The proliferation of exponential technologies can drive unprecedented opportunities for organizations aiming to create new business ventures and technology-based innovations. This may redefine what it takes to become a market leader where not size and past success and track record, but agility and networked access to resources and knowledge makes the difference. With the pace of technological change accelerating, as opposed to a 10 percent improvement in efficiency, which is insufficient, incumbent organizations must target to generate a *10× impact*. The potentially exponential trends or growth trajectories will quickly outpace a linear growth path. This clearly demonstrates the unlimited potential from the new exponential technology paradigm.

The new paradigm promises to contribute substantially with sustainable solutions to some of the world's most pressing challenges (e.g., poverty, climate change). In fact, when these technologies are used in combination to deal with complex challenges, they hold a much higher likelihood of developing sustainable solutions by making them:

- More creative with the ability to deal with issues we could not resolve before
- Easier by making complex, laborious tasks almost effortless
- Faster by rapidly diffusing and scaling new capabilities globally
- Cheaper with an exponential drop in costs as technologies become more powerful
- Better and more effective in generating new capabilities

## Genesis of Startups

In the second half of the 19th century, the first structure for innovation formed was called research and development (R&D) organization with the aim of developing novel socioeconomic *applications* on a continuous generation of technological innovations. This was financed by industrial capital, which was typically focused on a particular domain of industry and was carried under conditions of competition and secrecy of development. This involved two major inflows, the first based on industrial capitals and the second based on scientific knowledge as well as successful and failed socioeconomic projects. Industrial capitals financing R&D projects normally have the objective of obtaining a return of investment (ROI) that exploits the use of new technologies in socioeconomic projects. Manhattan Project for development of atom bomb at Las Alamos and Palo Alto Research Center (PARC) of Xerox are examples of R&D organizations.

Since 1970s, the emergence of venture capital startup (VCS) system in the Silicon Valley represented the alternative distributed approach to obtain new technologies accompanied by the development of new business models as also new financing innovations (Bonomi 2020). But, Georges Doriot was the founder of the modern VC industry (Ante 2008). The VC industry began to take shape after World War II on the northeastern seaboard when in 1946, Georges Doriot became the president of the first public VC firm: Boston-based American Research and Development Corporation (ARD).

Business model (BM) activity in a startup consists of the following activities:

- Articulate the value created for users and structure of the value chain, that is, network of firm's activity required to create and distribute products or services or experiences to customers
- Identification of a market segment in which technology is useful and for what purpose
- Estimate cost structure and profit potential, and formulate the competitive strategy by which the innovating technology would gain and hold advantage over rivals

The VCS system has the objective of obtaining an ROI by selling the developed technologies, and with resulting ROI, refinancing new technology developments through newer startups. In this manner, after a part made available to the startup founders and retention of part of ROI as reward by VC, when ROI is majorly positive, an autocatalytic cycle of investments and reinvestments gets initiated. The objective of a startup is reaching an exit that normally consists of selling of the developed technology typically to a great company, or of collecting capital by being quoted in a stock exchange, in order to become an industrial company.

> Although startups are organized legally as companies, in fact, their activity is more like that of a project(s) defined as a one-of-a-kind activity undertaken to achieve an objective within a time limit and budget that is derived by their capitalization.

Market knowledge is considered of main importance and market risks considered more significant than the technical risks in the startup activity. In order to be successful, VC portfolios cannot consider a high number of startups, such as that required per a portfolio strategy. Portfolio strategies, largely used in financial activities, are of limited value to a VC—not only in mitigating the downside risks inherent in science-based innovation projects but also in enhancing the probability of exceptional rewards. The alternative to portfolio strategy is to build a system of innovation designed primarily to:

- Maximize the probability of success for each project
- Limiting risk by selection of people in whom VC have confidence in both the technical and the business aspects of the venture

## Unicorns as the Confluence of Exponentials

Aileen Lee, founder of the U.S.-based VC firm Cowboy Venture, coined the term *unicorn* in 2013, in an article titled *Welcome to The Unicorn Club: Learning from Billion-Dollar Start-Ups*. The term is given to companies based on their growth opportunities as well as their expected development. Three common categories exist under which companies are listed based on their valuation: unicorn includes businesses valued at U.S.$1 billion and over; decacorn includes businesses valued at U.S.$10 billion and over, while hectocorn includes businesses valued at U.S.$100 billion and over (PAUL et al. 2010).

Unicorns are the outcome of a confluence of triple exponentials, namely, exponential scalability along the dimensions of desirability, feasibility, and viability (DFV).

1. Internet-based applications that bring network effect and exponential value generation and capture in play ensure exponential desirability.
2. Cloud-based applications with exponential scalability in storage and processing resources that bring exponential feasibility in play ensure exponential feasibility.
3. AI-based applications that bring exponential cognitive advantage in play ensure exponential economic viability.

---

Internet as a new platform for business has had a profound impact on business ecosystems. Consider the value chain for traditional consumer markets: a value chain typically comprised three stages or groups of actors, namely, supplier–manufacturers (who produced the goods, or the parts needed to produce the goods), distributors (who moved the goods from producer to retailers), and retailers (who sold the goods to end users). An effective way for a corporation to succeed was to gain a monopoly in one of these three stages or to integrate at least two of the three stages:

- A common strategy was to take control of the distribution stage and then leverage that control to integrate backward with supplier–manufacturers who needed access to distribution channels to get their products to end users.
- Retailers could employ a similar strategy of leveraging their control over retail infrastructure to take control of distribution and (ultimately) manufacturing.

Either way, economic power was derived from the control of the supply chain.

The Internet makes the direct distribution and retail of information, products, and services effectively free (in the case of digital goods—software or data) or significantly cheaper (in the case of old-world goods that can now be sold directly to users online). Consequently, the advantage that the intermediary corporations traditionally enjoyed by reason of their control of distribution or retail gets reduced drastically.

Per the DFV hypothesis, the solutions developed with the help of AI are:

i. Exponentially desirable by the target groups and, more generally, by the society
ii. Exponentially feasible technologically and scalable applications that meet legal and regulatory requirements
iii. Exponentially viable by either generating more revenue or saving costs

As stated earlier in the *Artificial Intelligence as an Exponential Technology* subsection, AI (i.e., AI/ML/DL) has the best potential to shoulder the responsibility to continue the progress of Moore's law, albeit for an enlarged time cycle of (say) 2.5 years.

### India Startup Ecosystem

The world's seven largest firms in terms of market capitalization are Apple, Microsoft, Amazon, Alphabet, Alibaba, Facebook, and Tencent. It is usually assumed that digital companies dominate globally by ruthlessly exploiting early mover advantages, winner-take-all dynamics, tipping points, economies of scale, and network effects. But, in reality, most of them fail to reach anything that approaches global ubiquity. Amazon accounts for just over half of the digital market in the United States, but only about 6 percent globally—Amazon can reach half of humanity in about 60 percent national markets only. This clearly highlights location dependence of intangible products and services!—whose reach can be improved further through partner networks. This further highlights the potential of the Indian economy with a catchment area of 1.4 billion people within the national boundaries to launch, support, and nurture multiple high-tech startup ecosystems.

> The geographical effect of digital technologies is not to kill distance or to annihilate space, but to make space become more *sticky* as capital investment responds to lower labor costs, new infrastructure, and pools of skilled workers that provide opportunities for profit in some locations more than in others. If telecommunication advances are the strongest annihilators of the tyranny of distance, then economic activity should be increasingly dispersed to lower-cost locations or economically attractive areas, often smaller places. On the contrary, the larger the city, the greater is the pool of talent, the volume and variety of supportive resources (including universities), the exchange benefits of the clustering of competing firms, the quality of conventional connectivity (e.g., airports)—in short, the conditions that engender innovation and productivity, despite higher costs (Ang, Chia, and Saghafian 2022).

Indian startup ecosystem is growing rapidly and is already the third largest in the world. This is primarily because of one decisive factor, namely, the cost of failure in India is low compared with competing ecosystems like (say) of Silicon Valley.

Additional details are available in the Appendix section (**A.1.3 India Startup Ecosystem**) available online.

## Innovation Gap in Life Sciences

Innovation in IT is speeding ahead exponentially in hardware, software, and networking. For instance, digital photography was first developed by Steven Sasson in Kodak, the company it went on to bankrupt. In the process, the technology has gone from delivering 0.01 of a megapixel for U.S.$10,000—via a device weighing 1.7 kg—to 10 megapixels for U.S.$10 and 0.014 kg! In short, 1,000 times the resolution for 1,000 less in cost and weight. A billion-fold improvement in performance.

Customers for IT innovations are enjoying faster, better, and cheaper products simultaneously, but in life sciences and biomedicine, this is far from the case. Too often, life sciences products make marginal impact, take many years to arrive, and end up costing more (Barker 2016).

In light of discussion in *Unicorns as Confluence of Exponentials* subsection, we can observe that life sciences products are not exponentially *feasible* and, consequently, not exponentially *viable*. Life sciences and biomedicine areas are devoid of the phenomenon of bio startups and blockbusters (akin to unicorns).

Additional details are available in the Appendix section (**A.1.3 Innovation Gap in Life Sciences**) available online.

> It is tempting to explore the possibility that the spectacular growth potential in high-tech or IT industry can be deployed to the benefit of achieving higher productivity in the biotech sector. This has already been employed to enhance the productivity in biotech through the strategy of bioinformatics (Hilbush 2021).

## Unicorns as the Engines of Growth in the 21st Century

Silicon Valley, located around the southern part of San Francisco Bay, is perhaps the best-known high-tech cluster in the world and *de facto* is considered as the standard for all the other high-tech clusters worldwide. Silicon Valley and, to a lesser extent, the Boston/Cambridge region sometimes known as Route 128, have been models for other regions that seek to enjoy innovation based economic development. The Silicon Valley model includes a set of institutions that promote new firm innovations: early VC financing, equity markets for IPOs of recently founded firms, fluid regional labor markets for global talent, fiscal policies that lower the costs of starting and operating a business, and proximity of university and research institutes within a region. The role of first-rate universities such as Stanford University, whose campus is located in the core of the valley, and nearby University of California, Berkeley, cannot be underestimated. Social networks of engineers, managers, entrepreneurs, and investors reinforced the research-oriented and entrepreneurial culture.

Other important factors are continuous interfirm mobility and networks of interpersonal relationships (Malecki and Moriset 2008).

To what extent can the model of Silicon Valley and its processes of entrepreneurship and innovation be replicated at other places? The economic factors that give rise to the start of a cluster can be very different from those that maintain it. The most difficult and risky part is to get the new cluster started. At that stage, traditional factors such as firm-building capabilities, managerial skills, a substantial supply of skilled labor, and connection to markets are critical for the takeoff of a high-tech cluster—as they were for the Silicon Valley 40 years ago. However, these initial factors are naturally different from those that would keep it going subsequently.

The abilities to remain entrepreneurial and innovate constantly will be essential for all companies in an innovation economy. Steiber and Alange's (2016) book imbibes results from a year-long study of Google's approaches to management (Steiber 2014) and finds similar principles being applied at companies including Facebook, LinkedIn, Twitter, Tesla Motors, and Apigee. By distilling on the aspects that work across a variety of innovative firms, the authors present a synthetic characteristics of a Silicon Valley company. The present book concludes on the same set of characteristics (and much more), addressed by the 9S model, by merely identifying the startup's overarching aspiration for metamorphosizing into an exponential organization or a unicorn. As highlighted in this book's *Abstract*, the very aim of attaining a unicorn status dictates characteristics of the strategy, structure, and operations of the startup. This also immediately explains why the Google model is applicable to other companies like Facebook, LinkedIn, Twitter, and so on: they all have one significant thing in common—they all had targeted to transform into an exponential organization or a unicorn.

Clusters in high-tech sectors are less common than in other fields: they are found mainly in large cities and university towns, and rarely in rural areas or in industrial cities. The high-tech innovation system relies more on VC and entrepreneurship (including serial startups and incubators), and much less on public sector bodies than in the *normal* regional innovation system. Because private VC is so central to innovation and entrepreneurship, the landscape of such clusters will continue to be uneven.

Only a small number of places have the network architecture, culture of innovation and entrepreneurship, and a knowledge base to attract global companies on a scale to rival Silicon Valley. Under such circumstances, while industrial clusters were the engines of growth in the 20th century, only a group of unicorns can be engine of growth, wealth, and employment in the 21st century.

## Conclusion

This chapter set the context for the whole book by establishing the rationale for the very search for exponentials. Moore's law that powered the growth during the Third Industrial Revolution (1969–2000) set the benchmark for expectations of growth for the next industrial revolution. The mantle for powering the Fourth Industrial Revolution with exponential growth falls on the class of intelligent systems, which includes artificial intelligence (AI), machine intelligence (ML), and deep learning (DL). The latter half of the chapter introduced the genesis of startups and unicorns emerging from the confluence of exponentials of DFV within a startup. The proposed DFV hypothesis for emergence of unicorns was applied to explain the innovation gap in the area of life sciences. In analogy with the industrial clusters in the earlier century, the chapter ended by recognizing unicorns as the engines of growth for the 21st century.

*This chapter highlighted how the Third Industrial Revolution in the 20th century was powered by Moore's law and industrial clusters were the growth engines of the world economy in the 20th century. It proposed that the Fourth Industrial Revolution in the 21st century will be powered by AI systems, and unicorns employing AI systems would be the growth engines of the world economy in the 21st century. Hence, the search for the exponential unicorns.*

# CHAPTER 2

# Startup Financing

## Topics Covered

- Methods of Startup Financing
- Startup Lifecycle
- Capital Budgeting Models
- Venture Capital Financing
  - Investment Models
  - Investment Priorities
- Term Sheet
- Startup Valuation
- Capitalization Tables
- Startup Exit Valuation at the point of acquisition or initial public offering (IPO)

## Introduction

*This chapter describes the startup lifecycle and associated aspects related to venture capital (VC) financing. It explains the investment models and priorities as also the startup valuation and related capitalization tables. It explains how the VC's investment model typically renders unicorn aspirations for startups inevitable.*

## Methods of Startup Financing

There are seven main methods of financing for a growing business (Feldman 2013).

### Bootstrap

Bootstrapping in most entrepreneurs' minds encompasses any technique short of selling equity in the company to outside investors. Bootstrapped companies usually begin with the founders pooling their financial resources. These resources may range from personal savings and second mortgages on the founders' homes to taking on credit card debt. Bootstrapping strategy may also involve direct bank loans.

> Creative bootstrappers are ingenious at getting company financing from wherever they can. This may range from prepayment of advanced product orders to government programs, which are discussed next.

The clear advantage often cited in favor of this financing technique is that the founders retain ownership and control of the company. While this method works suitably for low-capital or niche business, the company growth can ultimately be slowed by the inherently limited resources that founders can marshal. High-growth potential companies attempting to bootstrap may often underperform their potential due to such financing limitations. Moreover, this often entices other *fast follower* companies to seize such market opportunities unearthed by the original startup.

### Government Financing

The U.S. Government's Small Business Administration Small Business Innovation Research Program (SBIR) and the Small Business Technology Transfer Research Program (STTR) are the largest government grant programs for technology-based startups and the most frequently used by technical entrepreneurs. SBIR funds the critical startup and development stages, and it encourages the commercialization of the technology, product, or service, which, in turn, stimulates the U.S. economy.

### Bank Financing

Bank loans, including revolving lines of credit, are fairly easy to attain for profitable ongoing concerns. Bank loans need to be supported by collateral in the form of some company asset—nonfixed assets, such as inventory or cost receivables, can also be used as collateral.

But, entrepreneurs just launching a company typically cannot get a bank loan without putting up some personal assets as collateral, such as their house. Beyond the lack of availability, the other significant downside to bank loans for a startup company is the loan repayment schedule. Making regular loan payments may prove challenging for a company with no established or regular income.

### Friends and Family

Founders seeking this type of financing often seek it in the form of long-term loans. From a strictly business perspective, the interest rates on these loans should be well in excess of what the investors could obtain at their bank or in low-risk money market investments—but it may be easier to access.

### Equity Financing

Equity financing entails selling a portion of your company in exchange for cash. Unlike loans that can get paid from the cash generated by the profitable operations of the company, a private company's equity—an illiquid asset—can only be turned into cash or some other liquid asset.

### Acquisition

One way to transform private equity is to sell the entrepreneurial company to another entity for cash or publicly traded stock. As these investor groups will not want to have their investment tied up forever, the entrepreneur seeking this type of financing should anticipate the sale of the startup in well under 10 years.

The two primary groups that make equity investments in private companies are:

1. Angel Investors: Angel investors investing individually or in groups provide a significant amount of capital at the start-up and early growth stages. Angel investors can be more patient in their investment horizons and can wait for a period of 7 to 10 years before cashing out.

   The typical club or network process is that you send the required form to the designated club member. Following initial screening, if the entrepreneur is chosen, then follow-up meetings with several club members occur. If the entrepreneur is selected to present at a future meeting, then the entrepreneur is provided guidance in terms of business plan refinement and the presentation. Usually 12 to 30 minutes are allocated for a presentation and questions, and then any interested club members meet with the entrepreneur to discuss further steps in the investment decision process.

Startups can leverage five key enablers:

i. Team: refers to the distinguishing set of competencies, skills, and experiences that characterize the entrepreneurial team, together with the motivation and passion of each member, and their full-time engagement in the development of the entrepreneurial idea, in the final aim to strive relentlessly for the success of the startup.

ii. Time: refers to the team's capacity to monitor carefully this critical variable for the development of the entrepreneurial idea, by promoting a lean approach based on iterative cycles of key activities such as build, use, measure, learn, improve, and scale, in the final aim to show the traction of the startup, for example, how the number of customers increases over time.

iii. Target: refers to the methodological approach followed to identify and involve since the beginning the target customers, by structuring with them a durable and trustful relationships useful to develop and innovate continuously the company offering (product, service, or experience), in the final aim to deliver best match offer for customer requirements along with network partners.

iv. Technology: refers to the systematic process of continuous updating and scenario scanning about the technologies that are beyond the company offering and related business models, in the final aim to obtain strategic insights at technological and managerial level for envisioning and exploring new developments for the offer (product, service, or experience) and the market.

v. Talent: refers to the time and importance reserved by the founders to meet and discuss with experts, mentors, entrepreneurs, investors, and so on, to listen to their feedback and collect their suggestions, in the final aim to nurture and cultivate the talents of each member of the team and discover new talents to involve into the company development plans.

2. Venture Capitalists: Venture capital (VC) is a professionally managed pool of equity capital formed from the resources of wealthy individuals or institutions who are limited partners (LPs). Other principal investors in VC limited partnerships are pension funds, endowment funds, and foreign investors. VC is managed by a general partner (GP) in exchange for a percentage of the gain realized on the investment and a fee. VC can best be characterized as a long-term investment usually occurring over a five- to seven-year period—the investments are usually in second- and third-stage deals and leveraged buyouts. The venture capitalist will often provide debt along with equity in the financing. In each investment, the venture capitalist takes an equity participation through stock, warrants, and/or convertible securities and has an active involvement in the monitoring of each portfolio company, bringing investment, financing planning, and business skills to the firm.

The process starts with the VC firm establishing its philosophy and investment objectives. The firm must decide on the following:

- Portfolio mix (including the number of startups, expansion companies, and management buyouts)
- Types of industries
- Geographic region for investment
- Product or industry specializations.

The VC process can be broken down into four primary stages:

1. First stage is the preliminary screening, which begins with the receipt of a good business plan. The venture capitalist then determines if the proposal fits his or her long-term policy and short-term needs in developing a portfolio balance. In this preliminary screening, the venture capitalist investigates the economy of the industry and evaluates whether he or she has the appropriate knowledge and ability to invest in that industry. The numbers are reviewed to determine whether the business can reasonably deliver the return on investment (ROI) required. In addition, the credentials and capability of the management team are evaluated to determine if they can carry out the plan presented.

2. The second stage is the agreement on general terms between the entrepreneur and the venture capitalist. The venture capitalist wants a basic understanding of the principal terms of the deal at this stage of the process before making the major commitment of time and effort involved in the formal due diligence process.

3. The third stage of detailed review and due diligence is the longest stage, involving between one and three months. This includes a detailed review of the company's history, the business plan, the resumes of the individuals, their financial history, and target market customers. The upside potential and downside risks are assessed; there is a thorough evaluation of the markets, industry, finances, suppliers, customers, and management.

4. The fourth stage of final approval, a comprehensive, internal investment memorandum is prepared. This document reviews the venture capitalist's findings and details the investment terms and conditions of the investment transaction. This information is used to prepare the formal legal documents that both the entrepreneur and venture capitalist sign to finalize the deal.

### Initial Public Offering

A second way is to take the private company public through an initial public offering (IPO) on a major stock exchange (NYSE, NADAQ, etc.). To be considered for an IPO, a company must be quite large (typically with revenues approaching a billion dollars and growing quickly). Growing a company to such a size can take much longer than the time the investors are willing to keep their investment illiquid. Consequently, IPOs are much rarer than acquisitions—vast majority of startups financed via equity financing are acquired.

## Startup Lifecycle

A startup is a temporary organization designed to seek out a repeatable and scalable business model. Besides scaling revenue growth, annual employee increase (approximately 20% ) is seen as a key feature of startups. Thus, startups are not merely newly created businesses, but organizations that aspire to grow big quickly on multiple levels, although this can take up to a decade.

The startup lifecycle that is closely mapped to the funding stages is described next (Mishra 2015).

> Neither is a company a larger version of a startup nor is a startup a smaller version of a large company.

### Seed Stage

Startups in the seed stage focus on developing their idea into a concept, discovering potential markets for it, creating an organizational shell for their company, and acquiring seed financing to fund it all. They have to cater to internal organization and external validation. Entrepreneurs evaluate the fundamental feasibility of an business idea by obtaining feedback from business professionals, potential customers, and technical experts. Investors at this stage mainly include business angels, incubators, and public subsidy programs.

### Startup Stage

Startups in the startup stage focus on prototyping that includes not only technical core features of the designs and products but also market testing. While physical products require manufacturing facilities, supply chain management, transport, and channels to deal with returns, digital products use the Internet to spread around the globe instantaneously. Entrepreneurs continue to rely on outside capital inflow to ensure its survival. Investors at this stage include business angels, early VC, and even corporate VC firms.

### Growth Stage

Startups in the growth stage focus on augmented demand creation, satisfaction, and management. Increased demand is generated because of heavy marketing, ramped up sales forces, elimination of competitors, and enhanced customer awareness. To satisfy this increased demand, the company scales its operations, especially its production. Consequently, user and/or customer bases and revenues grow rapidly.

VC firms try to invest right before and during this stage, as cash inflows often outweigh cash outflows resulting in a large appreciation of the startup's valuation subsequently.

### Later Stage

Startups in the later stage focus on reaching maturity wherein the core product(s) start generating predictable revenues. The venture's valuation does not increase as rapidly as it did during the growth stage; consequently, financiers will either push the company to become profitable in order to yield returns on their investments or exit.

Most common strategies to exit are IPOs or acquisition, for example, through a trade sale. Other scenarios include internal takeovers, for example, through management buyouts and so on.

## Capital Budgeting Models

The business case of the startup should contain the cost–benefit analysis. The evaluation point is to justify that the benefits have outweighed the costs. This section gives a brief on six capital budgeting models. These models are:

- The payback method
- The accounting rate of ROI
- The net present value (NPV)
- The cost–benefit ratio
- The profitability index
- The internal rate of return (IRR)
- The economics value added (EVA)

Additional details are available in the available section (**A2.1 Capital Budgeting Models**) available online.

## VC Financing

A VC firm invests in entrepreneurial companies, that is, startups with high growth potential in exchange for equity in those startups (Metrick and Yasuda 2011). GPs of the VC firms raise investment capital from other investors who become LPs in these VC firms. GPs make the investment decisions and often become board members of the startup companies after the VC firm has made an investment. VC firms usually invest *in syndication* with other firms because of the heavy time commitments of the VC firms in coaching and guiding their portfolio companies. While small firms may have one or two GPs, large VC firms may have 5 to 10 GPs. LPs are typically investment funds such as pension funds, university endowments, retirement funds, and wealthy individuals.

VC firms earn money in two primary ways:

- Management fee, which is aimed at administration of the VC firm. The management fee is a negotiated number between the VC firm (i.e., GPs) and LPs; it is typically around 2 percent of the VC fund per year.
- Carry is a percentage of the positive investment return that the VC firm receives from a specific investment. The carry is a negotiated number between the VC firm (i.e., GPs) and LPs; GPs typically receive a 20 percent carry on successful investments. However, VC firms do not share similarly in case of investments that do not work out profitable: there is no proportional loss for the GPs on a startup investment that goes wrong.

A VC fund will typically have a set target value (say, U.S.$500 million) and a fixed life (say, 10 years), that is, GPs will invest the money raised from its LPs in select startups and return its profits to those LPs within that 10-year window. Successful startups go through some kind of liquidity event—become publicly traded companies or be purchased—in order for the VC firm to transform their equity stakes in these startups into cash that they can redistribute back to the LPs.

### Investment Models

The manner in which VC firms make money is termed as the investment model. The venture capitalists' investment model is limited to a narrow band of companies whose growth can be greatly accelerated by a significant infusion of capital.

The major investment models are:

i. Conservative investment model: In this model, conservative returns are made by the venture capitalists by investing in startups that can result in conservative returns (say, two times) their investment.

ii. Home run investment model: In this model, returns are maximized by the venture capitalists by investing only in startups that can result in *home-run* returns (say, 10x) their investment, that is, have a huge upside potential.

Assuming that 100 percent of the investments in the conservative model are successful, the investment returns to both the LPs and the GPs of the VC firms would be almost 80 percent less than the investment returns obtained even by assuming only 20 percent of the investments in the home-run model are successful. This heavily biases venture capitalists to predominantly invest in startups that can potentially deliver huge upsides (i.e., by increasing their valuations by 10x to 50x or more)—that is, the reason why the home-run model dominates the VC industry. These startups (first investment to liquidation) must also fall within the timing window of the 10-year VC fund. This effectively determines a very narrow band of successful startups that are considered *venture backable* or *venture grade* by VC firms.

A VC firm typically sells their LPs on the concept that the fund yields a 35 percent return on their investment. Accordingly, each home-run investment must potentially return in far excess of the overall fund return target to cover the losses of the other investments. A fund making investments in 10 early-stage startups typically sees the following:

- One of their portfolio companies delivering tremendous returns
- Two or three of the 10 *going sideways* (returning their investment, plus a nominal profit)
- The rest going bust, being written off as total losses

> This is the root cause of the exponential aspirations that drive the search for exponentials (see Chapter 1 subsection *Unicorns as Confluence of Exponentials.*)

The success rate of these venture firms is measured by the IRR. The IRR is, by definition, the discount rate at which the NPV of their investment is zero. The IRR is the preferred measure of equity investors as it takes into account both:

(a) The amount of the return
(b) The timing (time from investment to cash out) of that return

However, the LPs do not turn over all the capital they have committed to the VCs firms at once, but do so whenever they receive a GP request termed as a *capital call*; the corresponding incremental infusions of capital into startup are termed as investment rounds that are ideally enough to get the startup from its current state to its next significant performance milestone while simultaneously containing the risks in five major areas:

- Industry
- Market/regulation
- Business/execution
- Finance
- Product/technology

For instance, if the next logical company milestone is to create a beta product, then the company is likely to be funded only the amount required to create and get potential customer feedback on a beta product. If that customer feedback is as expected, then follow-on financing will take the company to the next logical milestone (say, development of a commercial product). These company milestones are tied to each investment round and negotiated individually. In addition to having a different purchase cost, stock issued in different investment rounds will have other conditions, which may vary from one investment round to another.

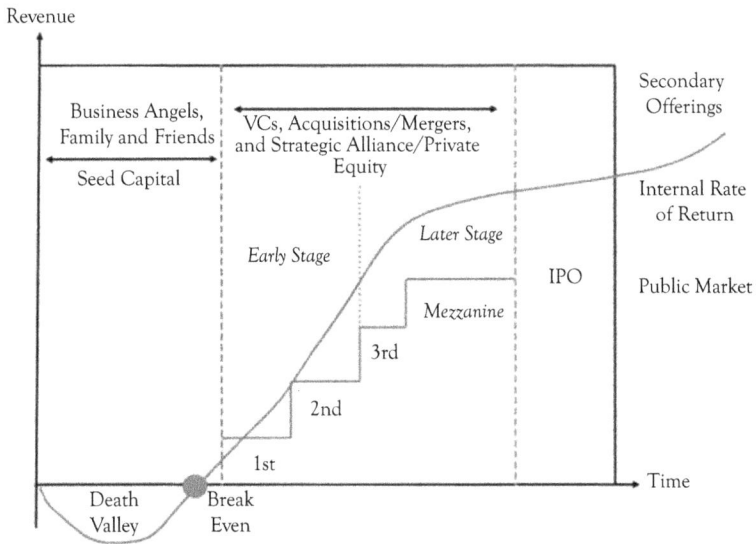

**Figure 2.1 Startup financial cycle**

For that reason, the issued company stock is kept track of and labeled according to the investment round in which it was generated (Figure 2.1).

*Series A* stock
*Series B* stock
and so on.

Each series of stock typically has a different preference with respect to the disbursement of funds in the event the company is liquidated. The original company's *founders' shares*, which are not associated with an investment round, are converted to *common stock* upon the first investment that triggers the issuance of a preferred series of stock.

After the frenzy of dot-com investments that went bad in 1999 and early 2000, VC investors attempted to reduce their investment risk by investing more heavily *downstream*, that is, at later stage investment rounds that required more capital. This shift created a dearth of investment capital in the pre-seed and seed stages. This lacuna has been attempted to be filled by angel investors, both individually and collectively (termed as *Bands of Angels*).

Equity investing requires a valuation of the company at the stage of the investment; angel investors and VC firms have long been at odds over valuing early-stage startups. Overtime, the compromise the two groups have arrived is that the angels do not attempt to value these preventure investments, instead preventure investments are typically made as convertible debt rather than equity—which are then convertible to equity at the stock price set in the first investment round of the VC investors (see *Startup Valuation* section). Consequently, pre-seed investments typically have IRR ranges from 65 percent and up—instead of 100 percent and up that would be more consistent with the enhanced risks associated with them. By contrast, the VCs argue that if a startup company is successful, the company will need further rounds of funding: the VCs will invest in all of these follow-on investment rounds, while Angels tend not to be invited to these downstream investment rounds. As a result of these investments in the ongoing rounds, the VCs will receive a rate of return for all their investments in a startup that blends the higher return rates for early smaller investment rounds with lower return rates for later, less risky but heavier, investment rounds. Early-stage funding for technology startups is still very difficult to obtain even today.

### Investment Priorities

VC firms investment priorities (reflected in the major risks areas enlisted earlier) vary markedly from that of the entrepreneurs, which are, first and foremost, typically focused on product and technology.

Most VC firms focus on investing in startups that reflect the expertise of their GPs, and that are also likely to receive follow-on investments. Successful startups tend to launch in low-volume, high-margin areas, and, as they grow, move toward lower-margin higher volume markets.

A VC firm's second priority for investment is generally the startup's team. Only a team can directly manage the execution, operational, and market risks that the company will surely face.

Thus, entrepreneurs seeking VC should:

- First and foremost talk to VC firms that invest in their space.

*Table 2.1  VC investment stages with corresponding IRR returns*

| Investment stages | Company focus | IRR returns |
|---|---|---|
| Seed | Concept exploration/development (e.g., beta product) | 80% and up |
| Startup | Commencing operations (e.g., commercial product) | 50–70% |
| First | Unprofitable ongoing concern (early sales) | 40–60% |
| Second | Growth of profitable company | 30–50% |
| Mezzanine or bridge | Bridge to IPO or sale | 20–35% |

- Next, they should emphasize the qualities of the team and their understanding of the space into which they are launching the business.
- Lastly, they should make the pitch for a specific product or technology.

Most venture firms focus both on an investment area (such as information technology) and an investment stage. Table 2.1 presents VC investment stages with the corresponding IRR returns.

If ML is usually applied to tackle prediction problems, can it not be useful in predicting the success of a startup (Ang, Chia, and Saghafian 2022).

## Term Sheet

Term sheets can vary depending on what type of funding round you are in, and how much is at stake, as well as who is involved (Metrick and Yasuda 2011). Generally, term sheets for seed rounds are going to be much lighter and shorter than for Series A or beyond.

Common items in a term sheet include:

- Who is issuing the note or stock
- Type of collateral being offered
- The valuation
- Amount being offered
- Shares and price
- What happens on liquidation or IPO

- Voting rights
- Board seats
- Conversion options
- Antidilution provisions
- Investors rights to information
- Founders obligations
- Who will pay legal expenses
- Nondisclosure requirements
- Rights to future investment
- Signatures

## Startup Valuation

As the startup moves toward commercial success, the startup risks are typically reduced with a concomitant reduction in the financing risk (Caruso 2020). Therefore, investors that invest at a later date cannot obtain the same rates of return on their investments as earlier-stage investors. As all shareholders at the startup's exit will receive the same share price, this implies that later-issued company stock is ideally sold to investors at a higher price per share than the earlier-issued stock.

A startup must be valued before it can be determined how much and for what price its equity will be sold. As share values for the startup are expected to change with each investment round, the valuation of the startup must be revised for each investment round.

For any given investment round:

1. *Premoney* value of the startup is the startup valuation before an investment is made.
2. *Postmoney* value of the startup is the startup valuation after an investment is made. The postmoney value is simply the premoney value plus the amount of the investment.

For example, a startup with a premoney value of U.S.$2 million that is accepting an investment of U.S.$1 million will have a postmoney value of U.S.$3 million. As the investor put U.S.$1 million into the startup and the postinvestment value of the startup is U.S.$3 million (m), then the investor just purchased one-third of the startup (U.S.$1m/U.S.$3m).

*Table 2.2 VC investment stages and median equity stakes*

| Investment stages | Median invest per round | Median premoney value | Median equity purchased per round | Entrepreneur's cumulative postinvestment ownership position |
|---|---|---|---|---|
| SEED | | | | |
| Seed | U.S.$1 m | U.S.$1.5 m | 1/(1 + 1.5) = 40% | 100% * (1–40%) = 60% |
| GROWTH | | | | |
| First | U.S.$4.9 m | U.S.$5.2 m | 4.9/(4.9 + 5.2) = 49% | 60% * (1–49%) = 31% |
| Second | U.S.$9.5 m | U.S.$18.2 m | 9.5/(9/5 + 18/2) = 34% | 31% * (1–34%) = 20% |
| LATER | | | | |
| Later | U.S.$12.1 m | U.S.$41.0 m | 12.1/(12.1 + 41) = 23% | 20% * (1–23%) = 16% |

Not all ventures move forward according to plan. In the ideal case, milestones are achieved in their expected timeframe and follow-on investments are made at higher valuations—and therefore higher per share prices—than previous round investments. This means that the premoney valuation in a follow-on investment round should be greater than the postmoney valuation of the previous round. This is termed as an *up round*. Development delays, poor customer reactions to proposed products, changes in the competitive landscapes or hundreds of other unanticipated occurrences could all negatively impact the future valuations of a startup. An investment round in which the premoney startup valuation is less than the startup postmoney valuation in the previous round is termed as a *down round*. The company devaluation will drastically reduce the anticipated returns on VC's investment (Table 2.2).

## Capitalization Tables

Capitalization tables, more commonly referred to as *cap tables*, track company ownership over time. They consist of information regarding the following:

- Who owns what stock
- What quantity of stock was issued

- When that stock was issued
- What price per share was paid for that stock
- What ROI is achieved by the all the investors

Some entrepreneurs get particularly fixated on the initial valuation of their startups. On the other hand, other entrepreneurs are fixated on the end valuation of their startups. Neither position could be further from the truth: all valuations impact the wealth that accrues to the founders. All premoney investment round valuations are critical to the founders and so are the postmoney investment round valuations for the investors.

Adopting the stance of a startup as a project, one can state that by estimating the exit valuation via comparison with an enterprise value (EV) of the public proxy company, one can apply earned value management (EVM) approach to estimate various elements of the cap table. Those elements are: exit valuation of the startup, the amount and timing of the required investments, and the intermediate company valuations. After reviewing these input variables, a model can be created that enables entrepreneur to obtain insight as to the economic drivers that create wealth for the entrepreneur and the startup. This model, upon which sensitivity analysis can be readily performed, will allow the entrepreneur to determine those variables that have the greatest impact on both the entrepreneur and the early-stage investor—including the intermediate-stage startup valuations.

## Startup Exit Valuation at the Point of Acquisition or IPO

Ultimately, the market—be it publicly traded stock or the value an acquirer is willing to pay—will set the exit value of the startup. While NPV-based valuations are best for ongoing concerns, the combination of the detailed information required for this analytical method and the disproportionate impact the terminal value has on the valuation derived from this method makes this approach impractical for startups. As entrepreneurs do not typically have access to private databases that contain data on the funding of private companies, a better approach would be to use publicly traded companies as value proxies for the startup company.

The weakness in using public companies as a proxy to value a startup is that one is comparing a fully operational company to an entity that typically has no product, no buyers, sometimes no clearly defined market, and an incomplete management team at best.

> The comparison can start with the kind of solution the startup is providing to customers and identifying other competing companies that are providing similar solutions. By combining the value captured for such solutions in the business landscape along with the estimates of the competing company's future estimated costs, the entrepreneur can estimate the kind of margins that can be realized by the startup.

Equity value, or market cap of a company, is the total value of the company as measured by the stock market, that is, the number of shares the company has outstanding multiplied by the value of the stock price of those shares. This value takes into account all aspects of the company. To be useful, the equity value needs to be distilled down to the enterprise value (EV) that reflects the contributions that the core operations has on that total equity value. For startups, the equity value and the EV are usually identical as startups typically do not have anything beyond their core activities. On the other hand, EV of a public proxy company can be calculated from publicly available financial information.

For its earnings before interest, taxes, depreciation, and amortization (EBITDA) to be suitable for comparative use with a startup, a good proxy company is the one that has a narrow operational focus and also has steady growth and investments over a period of time. Once a good proxy company is identified for the startup, the proxy company's EV to the EBITDA ratio can be determined. A further adjustment needs to be done for illiquid investments—investments that are difficult to readily convert into cash. When comparing public companies to private ones, the rule of thumb among many venture investors is that an equivalent private company will be valued 30 percent less than its public company counterpart because the public company stock can be sold easily, whereas the private company stock cannot be.

In summary, from the stock market, the EV of the public proxy company is determined. This public proxy company's $EBITDA_p$ value is derived from the income statement to yield an EV-to-EBITDA$_p$ ratio $p$. However, in order to compare this public company to the startup private company, this needs to be compensated for the nonliquidity of the private company. Using the 30 percent illiquidity valuation penalty results in using an EV-to-EBITDA ratio of ($p$ * 0.3) when estimating the exit value of the startup company. Obtaining the latest EBITDA$_s$ of the startup, the exit value of the startup can be calculated as ($p$ * 0.3) * EBITDA$_s$.

## Conclusion

This chapter described the startup lifecycle and associated aspects related to VC financing. It briefly described the seven methods of startup financing, namely, bootstrap, government funding, bank financing, friends and family, equity financing, and acquisition. It then discussed the various aspects of VC financing, including investment models, investment priorities, valuation, and capitalization tables. The chapter also explained why and how the *home-run investment model* is at the root of the exponential aspirations that drive the very search for exponentials. The details of the agreement between the VC and startup are detailed in the term sheet.

*This chapter explained how the VC's investment model typically renders unicorn aspirations for startups inevitable.*

# CHAPTER 3

# Startup Excellence

## Topics Covered

- The McKinsey 7S Model
- The Extended 9S Model
  - Shared Values
  - Strategy
  - Style
  - Stuff
  - Structure
  - Staff
  - Skills
  - Systems
  - Security
- Financial Analysis for Business Excellence
  - Financial Statements
  - Financial Analysis
    - *Ratio Analysis*
- Performance Management for Business Excellence

## Introduction

*This chapter sets the operative framework for the remaining part of the book. It describes the extended 9S model framework for business excellence—consisting of shared values, strategy, style, stuff, structure, staff, skills, systems, and security. It explains the distinction between (say) shared values and style or strategy and structure, which seem to have overlapping aspects that are sometimes confusing.*

# The McKinsey 7S Model

This section introduces the McKinsey 7S Model that was created by the consulting company McKinsey and Company in the early 1980s. Since then it has been widely used by practitioners and academics alike in analyzing hundreds of companies. We explain each of the seven components of the model and the links between them.

The McKinsey 7S model was named after a consulting company, McKinsey and Company, which has conducted applied research in business and industry. All of the authors worked as consultants at McKinsey and Company; in the 1980s, they used the model to analyze over 70 large enterprises. The McKinsey 7S framework was created as a recognizable and easily remembered model in business. The seven variables, which the authors term *levers*, all begin with the letter *S*.

These seven variables include structure, strategy, systems, skills, style, staff, and shared values. Structure is defined as the skeleton of the company or the organizational chart. The authors describe strategy as the plan or course of action in allocating resources to achieve identified goals over time. The systems are the routine processes and procedures followed within the company. Staff are described in terms of personnel categories within the company (e.g., engineers), whereas the skills variable refers to the capabilities of the staff within the company as a whole. The way in which key managers behave in achieving organizational goals is considered to be the style variable; this variable is thought to encompass the cultural style of the company. The shared values variable, originally termed superordinate goals, refers to the significant meanings or guiding concepts that organizational members share. The shape of the model was also designed to illustrate the interdependency of the variables. This is illustrated by the model also being termed as the *Managerial Molecule*. While the authors thought that other variables existed within complex companies, the variables represented in the model were considered to be of crucial importance to managers and practitioners (Peters and Waterman 1980).

Figure 3.1 depicts the interdependency of the elements and indicates how a change in one affects all the others.

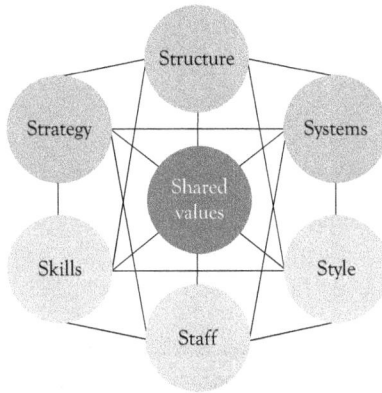

*Figure 3.1 The McKinsey 7S model*

The seven elements of McKinsey 7S model are described as follows:

i. Strategy: The plan devised to maintain and build competitive advantage over the competition.

ii. Structure: The way the enterprise is structured and who reports to whom.

iii. Systems: The daily activities and procedures that staff members engage in to get the job done.

iv. Shared Values: Called *superordinate goals* when the model was first developed, these are the core values of the company that are evidenced in the corporate culture and the general work ethic.

v. Style: The style of leadership adopted.

vi. Staff: The employees and their general capabilities.

vii. Skills: The actual skills and competencies of the employees working for the company.

> The external environment is not mentioned in the McKinsey 7S framework, although the authors do acknowledge that other variables exist, and that they depict only the most crucial variables in the model. While alluded to in their discussion of the model, the notion of performance or effectiveness also is not made explicit in the model.

The seven components described earlier are normally categorized as:

a. *Hard* elements are easier to define or identify, and management can influence them directly: strategy statements; organization chart and reporting lines; and formal processes and IT systems.
b. *Soft* elements are more difficult to describe specifically and are less tangible and more influenced by culture.

The remaining four S are more difficult to comprehend. The capabilities, values, and elements of corporate culture, for example, are continuously developing and are altered by the people at work in the company. It is therefore only possible to understand these aspects by studying the company very closely, normally through observations and/or through conducting interviews. If the organization is going to be successful, these soft elements are as important as the hard elements.

Table 3.1 shows the seven interdependent factors of McKinsey 7S subdivided into the *hard* or *soft* elements.

*Table 3.1  The McKinsey 7S model hard and soft elements*

| Hard value elements | Soft value elements |
| --- | --- |
| Strategy | Shared values |
| Structure | Skills |
| Systems | Style |
|  | Staff |

# The Extended 9S Model

This subsection introduces the extended 9S model by explaining each of the elements of the model with specific reference to startups.

## Shared Values

The appropriate culture and beliefs that support the needs and environment of the startup. These anchor ideas about what are right and desirable. For contemporary startups, this has to focus on *mass innovation as the next level of customer centricity as well as highlights the drive for cognitive advantage that underlies the current overwhelming demand for intelligent systems.* The focus of shared values is to do *right* things. For example:

- Customer centricity
- Mass customization
- Sustainability

---

### Shared Values Versus Style

Although the *shared values* and *style* elements may appear similar, they are quite distinct from each other in the sense that they correspond respectively to *doing right things* to *doing them rightly*. While the former is under the scrutiny and assessment of society at large, the latter is under the purview of the relevant or reference group's assessment. They are similar perspectives looking at two different phenomenon.

---

### Strategy

This is the clear and communicated direction and goals for the startup supported by a coherent set of actions aimed at gaining a sustainable advantage over competition. For contemporary startups, this has to focus on the overarching significance of Built_to_Innovate, scaling, and continuous innovation. The focus of strategy is to get the right *map* per the topography of the market. The orientation of each other factor must be evaluated and changes introduced to ensure compatibility with this strategy finalized for the startup. For example:

- Digital enterprise
- Intangible capital
- Intellectual capital
- Intellectual property
- Digital business model
- Growth

### Style

This reflects aspects of culture that have been accepted for adoption within the startup. For contemporary startups, this has to focus on software

---

### Strategy Versus Structure

Although the strategy and structure elements may appear similar, they are quite distinct, in the sense that they correspond, respectively, to the *map* and the *territory*. While the former is under the scrutiny of different kinds of analysts, the latter is under the purview of the different kinds of surveyors. They are two disparate perspectives looking at the same phenomenon.

---

experiments, multiparadigm development, and nature inspired solutions and strategies. It is linked to the management paradigm—*the way we do things here*—the focus here is to do things *rightly*. For example:

- Contemporary software development
- Nature-inspired solutions
- Cognitive advantage
- Collaborative leadership

### Stuff

This specifies the offering provided by the startup. For contemporary startups, this has to focus on product/service/experience lifecycle management and enabling experiences with AR and VR. For example:

- Product
- Service
- Experience

### Structure

The management and overall organizational structure that are aligned with the existing strategy and envisaged needs of a startup. For contemporary startups, this has to focus on collaboration and alliance networks and networks of projects. The focus of structure is to get the right coverage for the *territory* per the topography of the market. For example:

- Organizational structure
- Virtual organization
- Network of projects

## Staff

The appropriate HR to meet the demands of the existing business and future strategy of a startup. For contemporary startups, this has to focus on team-based management (not HR), talent management, and employee engagement. For example:

- Team-based operations
- Team-based management
- Talent management

## Skills

The capabilities possessed by the enterprise as a whole as distinct from those of individuals. Some companies perform extraordinary feats with ordinary people. For contemporary startups, this has to focus on data science, intelligent systems (narrow AI, general AI, super AI, generative AI). For example:

- Design thinking
- Modeling and simulation
- Complex systems
- Development security operations (DevSecOps)

## Systems

These are the networks, platforms and ecosystems that are prevalent or accessible within the Startup for its operations and management. For contemporary startups, this has to focus on network, platform, and ecosystems. For example:

- Sensor systems
- Internet of things (IoT)
- Industry 4.0

## Security

These are the techniques and computer systems for ensuring security, privacy, and trust in operations and usage of a startup's systems and offerings.

For contemporary startups, this has to focus on governance, trust, security, and privacy. For example:

- Governance, identity, trust
- Security and privacy
- Blockchain technology

## Financial Analysis for Business Excellence

As the business scales up, startups need to communicate financial information in the form of financial statements both to attract investors and to report on their performance (Schmidlin 2014). Startups usually achieve this via a double entry bookkeeping software application.

Additional details are available in the Appendix section (**A.3.1 Financial Statements**) available online.

---

The investment industry has tended to apply the traditional performance measures—more suitable for the mature and established operating businesses—on to a startup. These measures are flawed to the extent that they are based either on aggressive metrics or conventional business measures that have only limited application in a startup environment. However, some recent developments have put the spotlight on profitable growth requirements for startups. The collapse of Silicon Valley Bank (SVB) and Signature Bank have highlighted the need for profitable growth on part of Startups. Unicorns are expected to maintain a profitable growth of U.S.$100 to U.S.$200 million to get included in an even more exclusive club of centaurs.

---

### Financial Analysis

Financial analysis deals with the assessment of the commercial viability, stability, and profitability of a business, a part of a business, or any other project of a commercial nature. Typical questions addressed by financial analysis include whether to continue or discontinue an operation, whether to invest to expand the scale of an activity, which new technologies to adopt, whether to engage in a research and development project, or to understand if additional funding for the business in the form of loans or outside investment should be sought (Bhimani 2022; Kuratko and Hornsby 2018).

As a business is likely to have competitors, financial analysis is frequently used to compare different businesses against each other. Moreover, the results of financial analysis are likely to play an important role in encouraging external investors to invest in a business. For listed companies, because disclosure of financials statements are obligatory, a surprising amount of information and insight can be extracted from such statements by outside parties using financial analysis techniques.

Financial analysis deals with four aspects:

1. Profitability: The profitability of a business constitutes its ability to generate income and grow in the short term and long term.
2. Solvency: Solvency is the degree to which the current assets of a business exceed the current liabilities of that business. Solvency thus reflects the ability to pay bills, meet commitments, and pursue activities directed at growth. Conversely, insolvency is a state of financial distress in which a business (or a person!) is not able to pay bills or meet other financial obligations. In this situation, a business may be forced to wind up, involving a process of voluntary or compulsory liquidation in which the assets the company owns are sold to pay for the business's debt.
3. Liquidity: Liquidity describes the readiness with which assets can be converted into cash. Holding liquid assets is important for businesses (and individuals) because they are the source of the cash flows required to meet any current and future commitments. Typical examples for illiquid assets include real estate, vehicles, antiques, works of art, collectibles, and shareholdings in businesses that are not traded on a stock exchange. Such assets may be difficult to sell readily due to a low volume of trading activity in the markets for such assets or simply because the number of potential buyers is small.
4. Stability: The stability of a business is its ability to continue operating in the long term. The characteristics of stable businesses are that they do not maintain excessive levels of debt, use assets efficiently in

their operations, and will return acceptable levels of profit. Stability refers to the ability to survive temporary problems such as periods of low sales, lower than ideal levels of funding, the unavailability of important equipment, or the departure of important employees. While stable businesses will usually hold liquid assets in reserve for such lean or disruptive periods, having a large number of long-term customers is considered the best protection against such instabilities of businesses.

Additional details are available in the Appendix section (**A.3.2 Ratio Analysis**) available online.

## Performance Management for Business Excellence

Enterprise performance management (PMS) is the use of quantified information about the efficiency and effectiveness of enterprise activities to effectively monitor, control, and manage the implementation of strategic initiatives, combining the business strategy and technological structure to direct the entire organization toward achievement of common organizational objectives (Venanzi 2012). A performance measurement system is a set of metrics used to quantify the efficiency and effectiveness of action, whereby a performing business achieves the objectives set by the leadership team. Performance is the action that achieves the objectives set by the leadership team.

### Performance Measurement Systems Models

This subsection presents briefs on a selection of performance measurement systems. Table 3.2 presents a comparison of these models in terms of the perspectives incorporated, corresponding categories of measures and generalized aspects of comparison in terms of:

  i. Measures at different business layers
 ii. Strategic measures expressed in objectives
iii. Measures reflecting continuous improvement
 iv. Operational measures linked to objectives
  v. Measures elaborating on cause and effect relations

## Balanced Scorecard

The balanced scorecard (BSC) was initially introduced in 1992 by Kaplan and Norton as a pure measurement tool. Eventually, it evolved toward a strategic management system that enables a company to link long-term strategy to short term actions. The BSC is a tool that adds value by providing both relevant and balanced information in a concise way for managers, creating an environment that is conducive to learning organizations and eliminating the need for managers to *choose* which type of control system to use at any given time. It contains outcome measures and the performance drivers of outcomes, linked together in cause-and-effect relationships and, thus, aims to be a feedforward control system.

The basis of the BSC lies around the use of four perspectives, namely, the financial, customer, internal business process, and learning and growth perspectives, to determine the business performance. Within this method, the company translates its vision and strategy toward concrete goals with appropriate indicators, showing the degree of achieving these goals. Figure 3.2 represents a schematic of the BSC.

## Performance Pyramid System

Performance pyramid system (PPS) was originally developed by Judson in 1990. The purpose of the PPS is to link an organization's strategy with its operations by translating objectives from the top down (based on customer priorities) and measures from the bottom up. The framework ties together the hierarchical view of business performance measurement with the business process view (Figure 3.3).

PPS clearly delineates two measures:

i. Those of interest to external stakeholders like customer satisfaction, quality, and delivery
ii. Those of interest to Internal stakeholders like productivity, cycle time, and waste

## EFQM Business Excellence Model

The introduction of the business excellence model came after the European Foundation for Quality Management (EFQM) was founded in

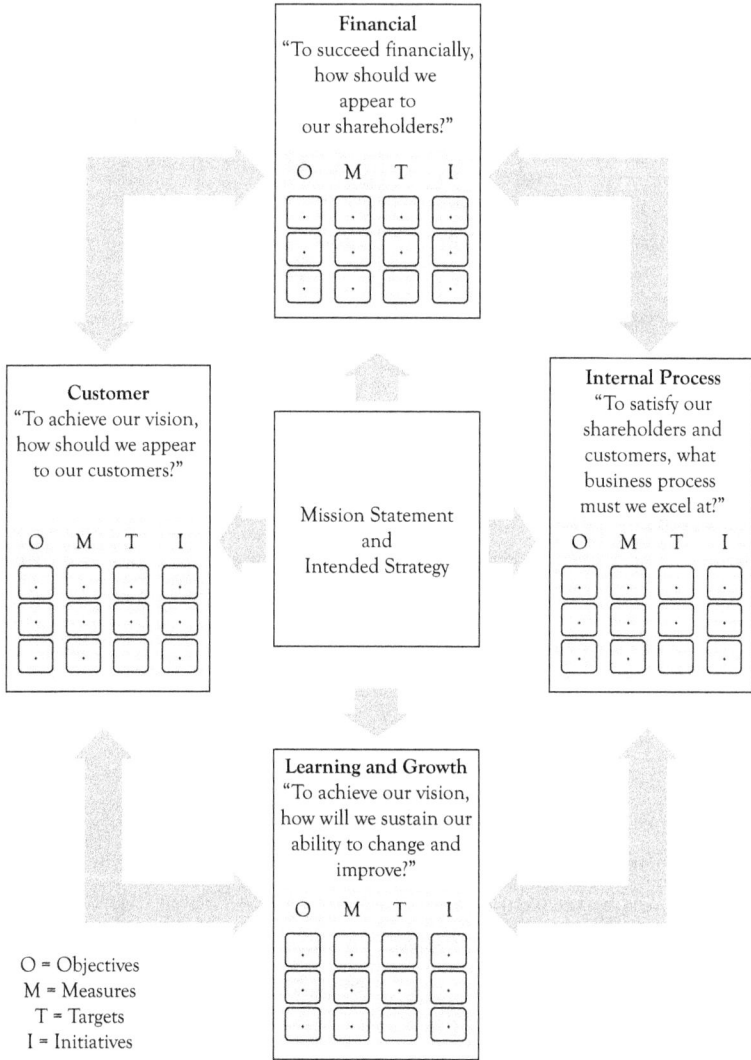

**Figure 3.2  BSC**

1988, set up by 14 major European companies due to a lack of quality, productivity, and competitiveness in a dynamic world market. It was used as the assessment model for the European Quality Award since 1991, and later transformed into the business excellence model, as shown in Figure 3.4. It consists of criteria a company can manipulate, the enablers, and criteria a company will achieve, the results.

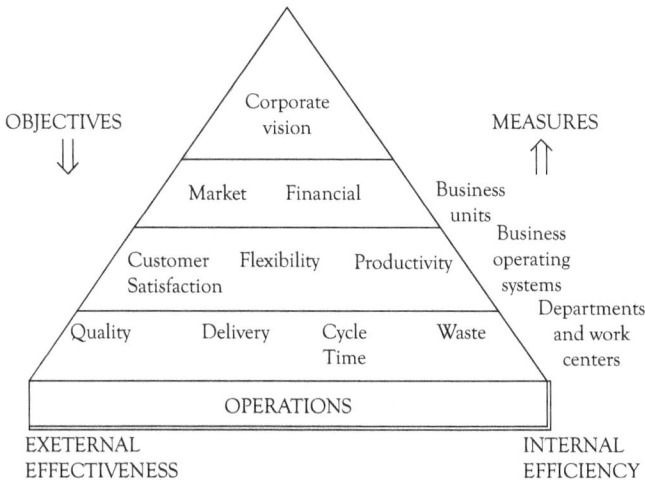

*Figure 3.3 PPS*

## Decision Support for Business Excellence

A decision is a choice from multiple alternatives, usually made with a fair degree of rationality. In an enterprise, these decisions may concern the development of a strategic plan and imply therefore substantial investment choices, the definition of marketing initiatives and related sales predictions, and the design of a production plan that allows the available human and technological resources to be employed in an effective and efficient way. For startups, the most significant decisions would be related to the focusing on a particular industry, the selection of the team and, finally, the offering (or product) (Mukherjee 2022).

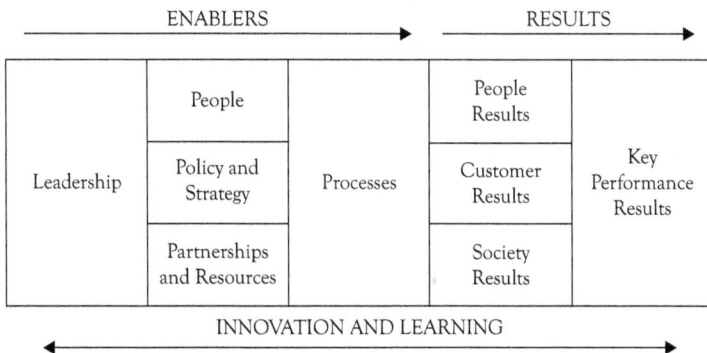

*Figure 3.4 EFQM business excellence model*

*Table 3.2  Comparison of PMS models*

| | BSC[a] | PPS[b] | EFQM[c] |
|---|---|---|---|
| **Perspectives** | | | |
| Enablers | | | ✓ |
| Results | | | ✓ |
| Financial | ✓ | | |
| Customer | ✓ | | |
| Suppliers | | | |
| External effectiveness | | ✓ | |
| Internal efficiency | | ✓ | |
| Internal business processes | ✓ | | |
| Learning and growth (innovation[c]) | ✓ | | ✓ |
| **Measurement categories** | | | |
| Financial (business results[c]) | ✓ | | ✓ |
| Revenue | | | |
| Cost | | | |
| Waste | | ✓ | |
| Customer (satisfaction[d]) | ✓ | ✓ | ✓ |
| Impact on society | | | ✓ |
| Quality (products[d]) | | ✓ | |
| Delivery (precision) | | ✓ | |
| Business processes (activities[d]) | ✓ | | ✓ |
| (Cycle[b]) time | | ✓ | |
| Flexibility | | ✓ | |
| Productivity | | ✓ | |
| Resources | | | ✓ |
| Learning and growth (innovation[f]) | ✓ | | |
| People | | | ✓ |
| Leadership | | | ✓ |
| Policy and strategy | | | ✓ |
| Competitiveness | | | |
| Environment | | | |

The decision-making process is part of a broader subject usually referred to as problem-solving, which refers to the process through which individuals try to bridge the gap between the current operating conditions of a system (as is) and the supposedly better conditions to be achieved in the future (to be). In general, the transition of a system toward the desired state implies overcoming certain obstacles and is not easy to attain. This forces decision makers to devise a set of alternative feasible options to achieve the desired goal, and then choose a decision based on a comparison between the advantages and disadvantages of each option. Hence, the decision selected must be put into practice and then verified to determine if it has enabled the planned objectives to be achieved. When this fails to happen, the problem is reconsidered iteratively.

Additional details are available in the Appendix section (**A.3.3 *Types of Decisions***) available online.

## Decision-Making Process

The nature of a decision process depends on many factors, like the characteristics of the organization within which the system is placed; the subjective attitudes of the decision makers; the availability of appropriate problem-solving methodologies; and the availability of effective decision support tools.

Decision-making processes consists of following steps:

1. Intelligence. In the intelligence phase, the task of the decision maker is to identify, circumscribe, and explicitly define the problem that emerges in the system under study. The analysis of the context and all the available information may allow decision makers to quickly grasp the signals and symptoms pointing to a corrective action to improve the system performance. For example, during the execution of a project the intelligence phase may consist of a comparison between the current progress of the activities and the original development plan. In general, it is important not to confuse the problem with the symptoms. For example, suppose that an e-commerce bookseller receives a complaint concerning late delivery of a book order placed online. Such inconvenience may be interpreted as the problem and be tackled by arranging a second delivery by priority shipping to circumvent the dissatisfaction of the customer.

2. Design. In the design phase, actions aimed at solving the identified problem should be developed and planned. At this level, the

experience and creativity of the decision makers play a critical role, as they are asked to devise viable solutions that ultimately allow the intended purpose to be achieved. Where the number of available actions is small, decision makers can make an explicit enumeration of the alternatives to identify the best solution. If, on the other hand, the number of alternatives is very large, or even unlimited, their identification occurs in an implicit way, usually through a description of the rules that feasible actions should satisfy. For example, these rules may directly translate into the constraints of an optimization model.

3. Choice. Once the alternative actions have been identified, it is necessary to evaluate them on the basis of the performance criteria deemed significant. Mathematical models and the corresponding solution methods usually play a valuable role during the choice phase. For example, optimization models and methods allow the best solution to be found in very complex situations involving countless or even infinite feasible solutions. On the other hand, decision trees can be used to handle decision-making processes influenced by stochastic events.

4. Implementation. When the best alternative has been selected by the decision maker, it is transformed into actions by means of an implementation plan. This involves assigning responsibilities and roles to all those involved into the action plan.

5. Control. Once the action has been implemented, it is finally necessary to verify and check that the original expectations have been satisfied and the effects of the action match the original intentions. In particular, the differences between the values of the performance indicators identified in the choice phase and the values actually observed at the end of the implementation plan should be measured. In an adequately planned DSS, the results of these evaluations translate into experience and information, which are then transferred into the data warehouse to be used during subsequent decision-making processes.

---

Decision theory (DT) refers to the process of selecting the most desirable alternative from a set of feasible options. It entails building a mathematical model that simulates the rational behavior of the decision maker. Such a model includes parameters that reflect:

- Decision maker's preferences
- Objectives of the decision process
- Constraints that limit the solution space

For multiple criteria, it is difficult and impractical to combine these various aspects in a single measure of utility. Therefore, multiattribute decision making (MADM) and multiobjective decision making (MODM) approaches (and corresponding software tools and applications) are needed to support the decision maker in the selection of the *best* alternative among a huge set of solutions. MCDM/MADM can be applied in a broad range of business areas such as customer offerings (products/services/experiences), financial management, project management, and energy management.

## Conclusion

This chapter sets the operative framework for the remaining part of the book. It introduced the McKinsey 7S model that inspired this book's extended 9S framework for business excellence—consisting of shared values, strategy, style, stuff, structure, staff, skills, systems, and security. Startups need to communicate financial information in the form of financial statements both to report on their performance and to attract investors. The latter part of the chapter described the financial statements, performance management systems, and decision support that are essential for ascertaining the business excellence of startups.

*This chapter explained the distinction between (say) shared values and style or strategy and structure, which seem to have overlapping aspects that are sometimes confusing.*

# CHAPTER 4

# Shared Values

## Topics Covered

- Startup Values
  - Culture and Trust
- Customer Centricity
  - Mass customization Business Model
  - Mass Innovation Business Model
- Mass Innovation
  - Standardization and Customized Innovation
  - Methodologies for Customized Innovation
- Cognitive Advantage
  - Human Augmentation
- Generalized Sustainability
  - Carbon Cycles and Carbon Credits
  - Global Commons
  - Complexity Debt and Complexity Credits

## Introduction

*This chapter discusses the shared values that are vital for the success of contemporary startups, namely, customer centricity, mass innovation, cognitive advantage, generalized sustainability, increasing complexity of enterprises, and offerings. It introduces mass innovation as the next level of customer centricity as well as the drive for cognitive advantage that underlies the current overwhelming demand for intelligent systems.*

## Startup Values

In a startup, as the business model takes shape and it becomes clear which types of business need to be accorded highest priority, both large and small values by which employees set priorities in making their decisions become consolidated. Every startup that endures for even a modestly short time develops a set of values and a culture (Edmonds 2014).

Corporate culture and values are among the foremost factors that motivate employees and encourages them to empathize with the firm's identity. If the executives are seen to embrace and embody these values credibly, they can succeed in uniting the company and its employees in a nexus of values that can foster higher levels of motivation, aspirations, and accomplishments. Values are abstract notions representing fundamental, central, and general objectives and guidelines pertaining to member conduct and coexistence in social groups. In a firm, these values create a foundations for employee's decisions and actions; values serve as standards guiding direction, goals, intensity, and means while undertaking any action. Corporate culture is a firm-specific phenomenon encompassing the values, senses of direction, and cognitive routines and capabilities shared, upheld and practiced by majority of the employees.

The best way to see a startup's values is to look at its history of past investment decisions. The streams of incremental investments decisions taken by a startup during a past period of time is fairly indicative of its focal values. Values determine the larger strategic decisions that senior management makes. Resources are the most visible of the factors that contribute to what a startup can and cannot do. In a startup, much of what gets done is attributable to resources, both tangible (people, equipment, technologies, cash flow) and intangible (product designs, information, brands, current relationships with customers, suppliers, and distributors). Values are the criteria that drive a startup's resource allocation process—the mechanism that defines which threats and opportunities the startup will pursue, and which it will not. A startup's values reflect its business model or cost structure because those define the rules its employees must follow for the business to prosper.

That is the root cause of its focus on sustainability issues of the business and business practices pursued by a startup (see *Generalized Sustainability* subsection).

Values define the standards by which employees set priorities that enable them to judge:

- Whether an order is attractive or unattractive
- Whether a customer is more important or less important
- Whether an idea for a new product or a new service is attractive or marginal, and so on.

## Culture and Trust

The founder usually has strong opinions about how employees should do their work and what the startup's priorities need to be. If the founder's judgments are sound, employees will experience for themselves and trust the validity of the founder's problem-solving and decision-making methods. Thus, processes become defined. Likewise, if the startup becomes financially successful by allocating resources according to criteria that reflect the founder's priorities, the startups' values coalesce around those criteria.

As the successful startup matures, employees gradually come to assume and trust that the processes and priorities they have used so successfully so often are the right way to perform their work and daily tasks. Once that happens and employees begin to follow processes and decide priorities by assumption rather than by conscious choice, that trust in those processes and values come to constitute the foundation of the startup culture. Such trust and culture is a powerful management tool in trying situations—it enables employees to act autonomously but causes them to act consistently.

A startup culture explains how people perceive the startup, and consequently determines how they behave. However, there is the potential for multiple and even competing subcultures existing within the startup, each different in some respects from each other and from the parent culture. And, in the absence of any dominant superculture, the various subcultures could well be in conflict with each other. The startup culture being controlled to make management's desired culture both coherent in itself and dominant over other subcultures is an essential quality of the excellent enterprises. Thus, a startup culture offers a way for people in the startup to focus their efforts consistently to achieve a sense of direction and achievement, beyond the scope of more formal management approaches (Emary et al. 2020).

---

The factors that define a startup's capabilities and disabilities evolve over time in a resources–processes–values framework—they start in resources, then move to visible and articulated processes and values and migrate finally to culture. As long as the startup continues to face the same sorts of problems that its processes and values were designed to address, managing the startup can be straightforward. But because those factors also define what the startup cannot do, effectively they are rendered as disabilities when the problems facing the startup change fundamentally. Changing such out-of-date values and, by extension, the collective culture is very challenging.

---

The extent of the cultural transition or transformation, if necessitated because of the changing circumstances, is as broad and comprehensive as the startup itself. Some critical aspects of the startup life that have practical cultural implications include:

- Communication as the nerve system of the enterprise
- Coordination, cooperation, and collaboration
- Conflict creation and resolution mechanisms
- Commitment and consent
- Cohesiveness and member ownership of enterprise aims
- Levels of acceptable caring and concern for others
- Trust

These operating processes interact to define the social aspects of the enterprise.

In summation, a startup's culture can be defined as the character of genuine commitment and order in employees, teams, and groups within the startup that allows people to trust in those processes and values that the startup has used so successfully so often that they give direction to its daily life and allow people to trust each other enough to work together.

Accordingly, trust is understood as the expectancy held by an individual or group that promises will be kept and vulnerability will not be exploited.

The development of trust involves being positively accountable for deviations from the expected performance. So long as those trusted behaved in line with expectations, trust would be reinforced as a result of experience and built progressively over time. It does not need to involve belief in the good character or morality of the other party, merely their conformance to agreed action (see Chapter 9, *Team Organizational Elements* subsection end box). The replacement of a command-and-control approach with a more democratic and communicative approach has to be based on establishing trust between the individuals and groups involved.

## Customer Centricity

The advent of the total quality management (TQM) movement in the United States led to the emergence of customer satisfaction measures, and efforts aimed at improving and sustaining them led to greater emphasis on customer centricity. The TQM turned attention to customer needs and forced a rethinking of traditional management methods.

Customer relationship management (CRM) is a different approach to business that involves relationship marketing, customer retention, and cross-selling, leading to customer extension (see *Customer Lifecycle* subsection). CRM represents a culmination of a long, evolutionary shift in the traditional thinking of business. Until the last few decades, the business of the global economy was, essentially, manufacturing. The focus on goods rather than services led to a product-focused, mass-market marketing strategy, resulting in a high cost of acquiring new customers, and a low cost for customers switching to other brands.

Additional details are available in the Appendix section (**A4.1 Customer Centricity**) available online.

### Mass Customization Business Model

Manufacturing started with an artisan making a single product for a single customer, and, as such, was recognized as craft production. Manufacturing continued to evolve in the late 1800s during the Industrial

Revolution, pioneering mass production at the beginning of the 20th century. Later, the market demanded more and more variety, forcing manufacturing to move toward the paradigm of mass customization: mass customization can be defined as the capability to produce personalized goods, with near-mass production costs and efficiency. Thus, mass customization in a way is similar to producing goods and services to meet an individual customer's needs but with near-mass production efficiency (Tseng and Piller 2003; Tsigkas 2013).

Mass customization was anticipated by Stan Davis in the book, *Future Perfect*, in 1987: "the same large number of customers can be reached as in mass markets... and simultaneously they can be treated individually as in the customized markets of pre-industrial economies" (Davis 1987). Pine, in 1993, introduced an industrial perspective in the newborn concept and defined mass customization as "providing tremendous variety and individual customization, at prices comparable to standard goods and services" to enable the production of products and services "with enough variety and customization that nearly everyone finds exactly what they want" (Pine and Davis 1993).

One of the keys to mass customization is the use of dynamic business networks within and among enterprises. These are formed out of a set of loosely coupled autonomous business process capabilities with a linkage system that allows them to be reconfigured instantly for any particular customer order. By engineering the flexibility of the processing units and coordinating the flow of resources (materials or services) between these units, the mass customizer can produce an almost infinite variety of base products or service, at a cost that is competitive when compared even with a mass producer. Whereas labor in the mass production design is organized to perform repetitive tasks according to a singular command and control system, the mass customizer organizes labor to routinely respond to an ever-changing set of rules and commands. The mass customizer organizes labor to work effectively in a dynamic network of relationships and to respond to work requirements defined by the dynamically changing customer needs. Although there is apparently a great degree of centralization in both of these

models, there is a fundamental difference in the nature of centralization: in case of mass production, all decision making is centralized,
whereas in the case of mass customizer, it is only the coordination and
control that is centralized. The mass customizing enterprises central-
izes the allocation of work to different processing units to produce the
customer's product or service order.

Mass customization production can be achieved with strategies such
as:

a. Provide quick response throughout the value chain. Reducing the
   time needed along a firm's entire value chain is known as time-based
   competition. Speeding up new product development and reducing
   setup time in manufacturing significantly decreases variant prod-
   uct-specific costs. Shortening the order-to-delivery cycle in marketing also lowers complexity costs by reducing final goods inventory.
b. Create customizable products and services. This method involves
   producing goods that customers can easily adapt to individual needs
   in a *self-service* manner. It changes the focus of development and marketing, while production and delivery remain almost undisturbed.
   Office furniture that can be adjusted and computer applications that
   allow users to create their own system environment provide examples
   of this widely employed method.
c. Provide point-of-delivery customization. As customers know best
   what they want, this method performs the final customizing step
   at the point of sale or delivery. For example, men's suits and eye-
   glasses are individualized to a customer's specific preferences right at
   the shop. This can be achieved for general products if a firm shifts
   the entire production process to the point of delivery; however, this
   would adversely impact the functioning of the whole enterprise.
   Hence, the method discussed here is more appropriate for products
   having (say) only one inherently customer-specific attribute on an
   otherwise relatively standardized commodity. In this way, the standard part can be manufactured centrally, while the customized characteristic can be produced at the point of sale.

d. Customize services around standardized products and services. A standardized product can be tailored by people in marketing and delivery before it reaches customers. For example, car rental companies add customized services such as express service and club memberships for frequent customers to their standard commodity service.

e. Modularize components to customize end products and services. This is considered as the most effective method of mass customizing products: Modularize components that can be configured to a large number of product variants. Economies of scale are achieved through the components, while economies of scope and customization are gained by reusing the components to create a large stream of product variants.

### *Mass Innovation Business Model*

In the experience economy, the next step in customer centricity would be to innovate the offering to meet the next level of requirements of the customer. A product is mass customized with services, services can be mass customized with experiences (see Chapter 7, *Experiences* subsection). Companies that are able to recognize this shift and adapt in time will be able to realize the positive effects of higher perceived value, satisfaction, loyalty, word of mouth publicity, and revenue growth—which come as a result of providing strong customer experiences.

This shift fuels the experience economy as less emphasis is placed on material success and ownership, and more attention is given to experiences (see Chapter 7, *Experiences* subsection) and emotions (Chandra 2018) (to gain mindshare—not unlike analogous gain in wallet share or market share). In addition, the society is becoming more affluent and sees improved socioeconomic conditions. According to Maslow's well-known pyramid of needs, higher economic success enables more and more people to satisfy their basic needs and to increasingly strive for higher-level pursuits such as psychological and self-actualizing needs (Maslow 1943).

## Mass Innovation

The more customized a product, the more customers are willing to pay a higher price because the product closely reflects their requirements.

As customer benefit increases, the price elasticity of demand decreases, which enables the producer to harvest the consumer surplus. The know-how necessary to maintain such a market position is an invaluable asset but requires continuous investments. Further costs are incurred by the large product variety, by increasing complexity throughout the value chain, by highly qualified personnel, and so on. This cost disadvantage can only be balanced by a higher price. Some of these negative cost effects can be balanced by the economies of scope that can be realized due to synergies while producing several products simultaneously. If those products have something in common (e.g., fabrication tools, R&D resources, etc.), the shared activities and assets can be *spread* across a group of products resulting in comparatively lower costs of production.

Pine and Gilmore described customer experience as the highest level of corporate development in their pioneering book *The Experience Economy* (Pine and Gilmore 2011). The development of the *experience economy* or customer experience as a central corporate key performance indicator (KPI) can be seen as a logical outcome of four forces, namely, completion, brand economics, society, and technology (Clatworthy 2019). In the times of interchangeable services, customers no longer use the price–quality ratio for their purchase decision but rather the (anticipated) price–experience ratio. In other words, customers tend to sum up in their minds the (positive and negative) experiences, like preferred color or music, they have or are likely to have before, during, and after purchasing (say) a company service at a certain price, rather than merely paying attention to the quality of the service. This implies a change of perspective for companies—from product and service orientation to a focus on the psychology of the customer.

## Standardization and Customized Innovation

An enterprise following a standardization strategy sells homogeneous mass products. Close relationships between customer and producer is no longer possible; products are not made-to-order but are made-to-stock based on market research estimates. As mass-produced, standardized goods cannot consider individual customer preferences, their product attributes are chosen based on an average of preferences taken from a large number of customers. As individual customer's preferences diverge from this average preference, the benefit provided by the product—and thus the price at which it can be sold—is much lower than in the case of customized innovation. The competitive edge of a mass producer is always based on price (Modrâak 2017).

By producing the same standardized product in large quantities, costs can be saved resulting from the following two effects:

- Economies of scale are achieved due to generally larger facilities (factories, call centers, inventory, etc.), which spreads a considerable fraction of fixed costs to a large number of product units.
- The experience curve effect states that costs drop by 20 to 30 percent every time the cumulative volume doubles. This is mainly on account of increased labor efficiency (resulting from learning), specialization and redesign of labor tasks, product and process improvements, and rationalization, such as introducing more up-to-date technology.

In contrast to standardization, an enterprise offering customized innovation products or experiences caters to a very niche customer base and tailors its every offering to the very needs and preferences or choices of one particular customer—the product is differentiated from competitors' by satisfying each and every customer requirement at that instance (Kahneman and Tversky 2000). Consequently, very close ties gets established between the producer and its customers and, often, customers coparticipate in designing the product and express preferences or choices on how this innovated product should be manufactured. A customized innovator's competitive edge is therefore primarily based on product attractiveness.

Table 4.1 summarizes the characteristics of standardization versus customized innovation strategies for products or market offerings.

### Methodologies for Customized Innovation

The established methodologies for managing customized innovations are described in Kale (2016).

*Table 4.1  Standardization versus customized innovation strategies for products or offerings*

| Characteristic | Customization | Standardization |
|---|---|---|
| Scope of offering | Specifications of individual customers | Average preference of a large number of customers |
| Number of customers per offering | One, or very few | Many |
| Contact to customer | Close; customer integrated in designing and producing product | Not or hardly established (anonymous consumers) |
| Product fabrication | After order | Before order; in stock |
| Source of information on customer requirements | Directly from customer | Market research |
| Similarity of products within line | No product the same; tailored solution; batch size one | All products the same; homogeneous mass product |
| Product variety | Very large | Only one product variant |
| Product attractiveness | Inherently high | Inherently low |
| Customer retention | High | Low |
| Costs | High | Low |
| Risk of substitution | Low | High |
| Competitive effect | Decoupled from competition due to product attractiveness and know-how advantage; opportunity to avoid price-based competition | Risk of price-based competition (especially for firms with low market share); market leader protected by cost advantage |
| Market entry barrier | Product attractiveness and know-how advantage | Cost advantage of market leader |
| Price range | Rather high | Rather low |

Additional details are available in the Appendix section (**A.4.2 Methodologies for Customized Innovation**) available online.

# Cognitive Advantage

In the year 1950, Alan Turing, an English computer scientist, put forward a question "Are machines able to think?" and he answered it by bringing the concept of Turing test. Turing test is a methodology to determine if a computer can think like human which marked the beginning of artificial intelligence. The reason for the primary focus on Turing test is the overwhelming inclination to emulate human cognition abilities, resulting in the underlying preference for human-centric information systems and decision support systems (Carter 2021). For instance, the primary considerations of traditional hard computing are precision, certainty, and rigor. By contrast, the principal notion in soft computing is that precision and certainty carry a cost, and that computation, reasoning, and decision making should exploit (wherever possible) the tolerance for imprecision, uncertainty, approximate reasoning, and partial truth for obtaining low-cost solutions. The corresponding facility in humans leads to the remarkable human ability to understand distorted speech, deciphering sloppy handwriting, comprehending the nuances of natural language, summarizing text, recognizing and classifying images, driving a vehicle in dense traffic, and, more generally, making rational decisions in an environment of uncertainty and imprecision. The challenge, then, is to exploit the tolerance for imprecision by devising methods of computation that lead to an acceptable solution at low cost. Soft computing is a consortium of methodologies that works synergistically and provides the *cognitive advantage* by enabling flexible information processing capability for handling real-life ambiguous situations (Kale 2019).

Similarly, as discussed in Chapter 10, *Chatbots and OpenAI GPT-3* subsection, a similar motivation has resulted in incorporation of an *attention* mechanism that mimics human cognitive attention: it looks at an input text sequence *simultaneously*, and, on the basis of probabilities, decides at each step which other parts of the sequence are contextual or relevant or important.

### Human Augmentation

Human augmentation is the technology that allows us to take us beyond our current abilities and power. Augmentations can be physical or digital. *Physical augmentations*, like bionic limbs, can improve the abilities of the wearer in a number of ways. Physical augmentations may include bionic implants, or organic structures made of titanium, carbon fiber, or even ceramics. Augmentations of this nature offer an incredible amount of potential, but currently do not provide the complete and seamless user experience that is essential. *Digital augmentations* are digital beings that physically resemble, work in many of the same ways as, and may even have the potential to interact with humans on a more meaningful level than humans can today (Kim, Davis, and Hong 2022; Ma and Spector 2022). Examples of digital augments include intelligent personal assistants like Alexa and Siri (see Chapter 10, *Chatbots and OpenAI GPT-3* subsection), and are collectively termed as *smart suits* or *augmented reality (AR)* (see Chapter 7, *Experiences* subsection).

Human augmentation technology (HAT) is a technology designed to make people stronger, faster, smarter, and more emotionally capable. HAT enables us to increase our capabilities and capacities by enhancing our cognitive capacities, physical capabilities, emotionality, and everything that is under our control. Computer–human interface (CHI) is a subset of HAT technology to interface the human brain with a computer in an interactive manner. CHI facilitates us to take some cognitive functionality and expand it to the third dimension, that is, physical presence. HAT, on the other hand, is using technology to enhance your body, sense of touch, movement, and cognition to be closer to the machine or computer (Albert et al. 2022).

The goal is that humans can come closer to the computer and CHI will be seamless, intuitive, intuitive, and intuitive. HAT faces the same challenges as computer technologies on the one hand (like data, security, privacy, speed, computing power), and on the other hand, limitations of the human nervous system.

## Generalized Sustainability

The rapid deterioration of the natural environment as well as concerns over wealth disparity and corporate social responsibility present fundamental issues for human society (Osburg and Lohrmann 2017). In order to address these challenges, sustainability has gained increasing importance in business. In addition, there is an increased cultural and legal pressure, which also leads to increasing emphasis on aspects of sustainability in businesses (Brinkmann 2016). One approach to tackle these challenges is given by innovative business models that include new strategies that enable mass customization of products for satisfying the specific needs of customers individually. This approach effectively curbs the detrimental tendencies of the *throwaway society* (Attfield 2021).

Additional details are available in the Appendix section (**A.4.3 Generalized Sustainability**) available online.

### Carbon Cycle and Carbon Credits

Carbon is most commonly present within the sedimentary rocks called limestone or dolomite. The principle mineral in limestone and dolomite is calcium carbonate. Carbon is present in all life forms, and it is a key element involved with the regulation of our climate. One of the great challenges of our current era is human-caused global climate change, largely due to our disruption of the carbon cycle by adding tremendous amounts of carbon dioxide into the atmosphere over the last several centuries. Carbon dioxide, along with methane, nitrous oxide, water, and other gases, constitutes a group that is known as greenhouse gases. These gases have the ability to absorb energy as heat and store it in the atmosphere, thereby warming it. We have added huge amounts of carbon dioxide into the atmosphere through the burning of fossil fuels since the advent of the Industrial Revolution.

> By studying samples of gases trapped in ice, it has been estimated that in the 1700s, the concentration of carbon dioxide in the atmosphere was approximately 300 ppm (parts per million). Now, the concentration is over 400 ppm, with most of the increase occurring after 1950.

The increase in carbon dioxide is believed to be a driving force in global climate change. Many of these emissions derive from the burning of fossil fuels, particularly petroleum and coal. Over the last few decades, since concerns about global climate change emerged, many have looked at reducing the use of these fossil fuels as a key strategy to slow down the impacts of greenhouse gases on the planet. Climate action plans to curb carbon dioxide emission are adopted at national, corporate, and community levels, which include realistic and measurable goals. Once the goals are established, a listing of policy or strategy changes is devised to achieve the goals, including green computing (Smith 2014). For example, a goal to become carbon-neutral may include a mix of strategies that could include:

- Purchasing carbon credits
- Developing renewable energy sources
- Improving energy efficiency

On the lines of *carbon debt* and *carbon credits*, we can also conceive of the concept of *complexity debt* and *complexity credits*, respectively.

### The Global Commons

All the people on the planet share one Earth (ED 1987). We are unlike any time soon to leave it to explore and colonize other planets. We have to find ways to survive on this planet without destroying it. Plus, we all share planetary resources, our global commons, and must find ways to protect them for the good of all. In 1968, Garrett Hardin wrote an article in the journal *Science* called *The Tragedy of the Commons*, which utilizes the village commons as a metaphor for our modern age. In the past, village commons were used for grazing animals. They were called commons because the community shared the space. However, if one individual grazed too many sheep, it would destroy the commons for the rest of the community, thereby creating a tragedy where the entire community is unable to use the space for grazing.

Hardin took that idea further and suggested that many in our society were depleting natural resources to the point that they were becoming unavailable or unaffordable to many in society. It is only through the management of the natural resources that we are able to maintain them. Without management, the resource can become exploited, which will lead to greater demand for the resource, which hastens the resource's destruction.

If exploitation proceeds out of balance with natural systems, humans can do significant harm to the planet through the very act of living and working on our planet. Jared Diamond explores this idea extensively in his book, *Collapse: How Societies Choose to Fail or Succeed*. He noted how the residents of Easter Island caused widespread deforestation of their home because they opted to cut down trees to use them to transport the famous Easter Island statues that rim part of the island's coastline. He points out that the society collapsed shortly after the deforestation of the island because the ecosystem that nurtured the society was destroyed.

### Complexity Debt and Complexity Credits

The term *technical debt* is a metaphor coined by Ward Cunningham in 1992 (Cunningham 1992). Technical debt arises when false or suboptimal technical decisions are made, whether consciously or unconsciously. Such decisions lead to additional effort at a later point in time, which delays maintenance and expansion. Such debt is found not only in the code but in all aspects of software development and is termed as software debt (Mariotti 2008).

Software debt accumulates throughout the software lifecycle whenever the focus is on immediate completion and changeability is neglected. The accumulation of debt does not impact software delivery immediately. At first, focusing on immediate completion creates a sense of rapid feature delivery with management, business stakeholders, and the team. Business stakeholders respond well to the pace of delivered functionality, and so the team attempts to continue this pace. What they don't understand is that this is only an illusion of speed in delivery (Osburg and Lohrmann 2017).

At some point, small forms of decay in software become large enough to affect delivery to a point where working harder and longer don't result in successful outcomes. Although teams complain about quality issues that hinder progress on feature delivery, the complaints are not taken seriously enough until the issues present visible business challenges. Communication of software delivery issues that lead to future business challenges is not easy when the focus is usually on developing new features for users. The communication problem is exacerbated with the further separation of business and software delivery groups in companies. Business people are challenged with the lack of transparency provided by software projects. They learn about critical problems too late in the software development release cycle to make appropriate changes to their plans.

Software debt is made glaringly visible when the team works on stabilizing the software functionality late in the release cycle. Integration, testing, and bug fixing are unpredictable, and the problems do not get resolved adequately before the release. People involved in the project stay late working to get the release out of the door. At this point, it is too late to pay back the debt accrued during relentless focus of feature development (see Chapter 10, *DevSecOps* subsection).

Software debt is constituted of:

   i. Technical Debt: These are the activities that a team or team members choose not to do well now and will impede future development if left undone.

  ii. Quality Debt: There is a diminishing ability to verify the functional and technical quality of software.

 iii. Configuration Management Debt: Integration and release management become more risky, complex, and error-prone.

 iv. Design Debt: The cost of adding features is increasing toward the point where it is more than the cost of writing from scratch.

  v. Platform Experience Debt: The availability of people to work on software changes is becoming limited or cost-prohibitive.

On similar lines, *complexity debt* arises when needlessly complicated decisions are made that lead to additional effort toward simplification and enhancing usability at a later point in time, which delays maintenance and expansion.

In analogy with *carbon credits*, *complexity credits* can be rewarded upon evaluation and assessment of information systems reduction or attenuation of complexity for achieving agreed standards of computational processing.

## Conclusion

A common set of values binds people together. A startup's values are the criteria that its employees use when making prioritization decisions. The TQM movement, with its focus on enhancing customer satisfaction measures, eventually led companies to put greater emphasis on customer centricity. Don Peppers and Martha Rogers pioneered the concept of one-to-one marketing made possible by the advent of computer-assisted database marketing. This encouraged the market to demand more and more variety—forcing manufacturing to move toward the paradigm of mass customization, which can be defined as the capability to produce personalized goods, with near-mass production costs, and efficiency! Industry 4.0 furthers the impact of the paradigm of one-to-one marketing inward right onto the production systems. Variety and complexity management are indispensable pillars for the further pursuit of mass innovation.

Complexity management not only deals with the proliferation of product variety but also with the proliferation of processes and resources in enterprises. Lately, manufacturing has been expanding its focus beyond the economic context onto its social and ecological contexts, motivating companies to move toward sustainable manufacturing. Thus, manufacturing now is increasingly confronted with many new *business goals* that are not only related to profits but also to higher societal-level life aspirations, as also sustainability aspirations for future generations.

*This chapter discussed the shared values that are vital for the success of contemporary startups, namely, customer centricity, mass innovation, cognitive advantage, generalized sustainability, increasing complexity of enterprises, and offerings. It introduced mass innovation as the next level of customer centricity as well as the drive for cognitive advantage that underlies the current overwhelming demand for intelligent systems.*

# CHAPTER 5

# Strategy

## Topics Covered

- Digital Enterprises as Built_to_Innovate Organizations
  - Strategy
- Intangible Capital
  - Intellectual Capital
- Scaling
- Intellectual Property (IP)
- Entrepreneurship
  - Ambidexterity
  - Strategic Innovative Entrepreneurship
  - Continuous Innovation
- Business Model
- Growth Strategy

## Introduction

*This chapter presents aspects related to strategizing for the success of the contemporary digital enterprises, including intangible capital, intellectual capital, ambidexterity, scaling, entrepreneurship, business model, and growth. It highlights aspects related to unleashing the unicorn, namely, Built_to_ Innovate organization, scaling, continuous innovation, and growth.*

## Digital Enterprises as Built_to_Innovate Organization

As the rate of change increases with increasing globalization, technological breakthroughs, associative alliances, and regulatory changes, firms have to look for greater agility, flexibility, and innovation from their companies (see Chapter 4, *Mass Innovation* subsection). Instead of pursuing strategies, structures, and cultures that are designed to create long-term competitive advantages, companies must seek a string of temporary competitive advantages through an approach to organization design that assumes innovation is normal, that is, Built_to_Innovate or transformable firms (Kale 2014). Thus, the need for on-demand innovation in organization structure and operations, and, excellence is much more a function of possessing the ability for fundamental changes. Firms need to be built around structures and practices that routinely encourage innovation and not thwart it, that is, projects.

Agile companies produce the right product, at the right place, at the right time, at the right price for the right customer. The difficult challenges facing businesses today require organizations to transition into flexible, agile structures like projects that can respond to new market opportunities quickly with a minimum of new investment and risk (Wells 2019). As firms have experienced the need to be simultaneously efficient, flexible, responsive, and adaptive, they have transitioned themselves into agile firms with small, autonomous teams that work concurrently, reconfigure quickly, and adopt highly decentralized management that recognizes its knowledge base and manages it effectively (Galbraith 2014).

## Strategy

The success of firms in the current dynamic and uncertain business environment is largely determined by the capacity of the organizations to respond to changes in the environment and to constantly work on the innovation of their strategic orientation. Development and long-lasting sustenance of competitive advantage can be expected by firms that can quickly either create or generate favorable changes or adapt or adopt to unfavorable changes.

In markets that are dynamic but slow moving without intense competition across the whole industry, strategy management can be adequately addressed by either Porter's competitive advantage or resource-based approaches. While the former advocates firms to repose faith in their core competencies, the latter advocates extended sustainability of their competitive advantage. Both of them tend to look at strategy from a long-term perspective and tend to encourage remaining grounded in the industries where they have been able to harvest above the normal returns.

However, in turbulent markets, these approaches require a continuous process of maneuvering, learning, and assessing performance. Competitive advantage is seldom sustainable for long periods of time and is best interpreted as a series of short-term temporary advantages. In such circumstances, firms not only have to focus on defending the current competitive advantage, but also be on the lookout for establishing the next competitive advantage. As the underlying decisions and tradeoffs are quite difficult to frame and implement, this engenders another dilemma called the *innovators dilemma* (Christensen 2000).

Innovator's dilemma is characterized by:

a. Incumbent failing to relook at the sources of competitive advantage and to the strategies that may have given them success in the past. The value of these assets and strategies within the new technology, strategy, or paradigm may not be very significant or even relevant.

b. Incumbent's inability to abandon an old strategy or technology because of previous investments that represent sunk costs. The marginal cost of producing additional copies of products based on old technology can effectively be much lower than switching to the newer ones with the new technology that needs additional investments. But assets connected with the old technology usually represent a sunk cost only in the short term because in the medium to long term, as they will have to be unavoidably replaced, the relevant cost will be more of a replacement cost. Thus, in actuality, the cost of remaining with the old paradigm may tend to be prohibitive.

c. Incumbent responding to the paradigmatic change when it is too late. With the focus on status quo in the early days of the paradigm shift, the new strategy or technology may represent low performance and may not appear to be a particularly credible alternative. But, while the old strategy or technology is probably reaching its limits of performance, the new strategy or technology probably still has plenty of upside remaining, and its sudden growth is likely to catch the incumbents by surprise.

It is not easy for incumbent firms to successfully deal with radical innovation. Thus, in the context of the present book's focus on startups becoming unicorns, radical innovation will succeed only if it is financed by the proceeds of the same old strategy or technology that will be replaced or supplanted by it. An ambidextrous organization is able to maintain its efficiency in the current paradigm at the same time readying itself to adapt for the future—the former is managed in a more formalized and standardized way, while the latter is coordinated with greater freedom (Smith et al. 2017).

Therefore, for a startup to target becoming a unicorn within a reference timeframe of three to five years, it is essential for it to operate as an ambidextrous organization. Ambidextrous organizations can develop new products or services or experiences for new emerging markets where speed, flexibility, and experimentation are critical, and also simultaneously compete in the competitive markets where efficiency, cost, dynamic innovation are critical. On the other hand, organizations that focus solely on one aspect (say) exploration may fail to adopt to changes in demand volume and prevent themselves from benefiting themselves from economics of scale. Organizations that focus solely on exploitation may fail to adopt to changes in requirements and prevent themselves from benefitting themselves from economic of scope.

In summation, organizational ambidexterity is the capability of the organization to maintain a balance between exploration and exploitation. Overall, ambidextrous organizations tend to perform better and thrive in business compared with nonambidextrous organizations.

## Intangible Capital

There are various reasons for increasing interest in intangibles (Moro-Visconti 2022):

1. Knowledge as the fundamental and major source of competitive advantage.
2. The widening gap between the market and book value for most listed companies. Especially for high-tech services industries, the measure of corporate assets is no longer per the physical paradigm.
3. Value creation is now the predominant measure of corporate performance.
4. Rapid ascendency of services as the predominant component of the gross domestic product (GDP) in most advanced economies.
5. Dematerialization of manufacturing industries.

Investments in creating and maintaining enterprise knowledge represents investment in the capability to create or enhance intangible assets (Cohen 2005). Information services (IS) and information technology (IT) are helping organizations to replace tangible with intangible assets, thereby increasing the proportion of intangible assets in the valuation of the organization.

The role and amount of intangibles is increasingly becoming larger to such a point that their value completely overwhelms the sum total of all other assets. An organizations intangible assets can be interpreted as the organization's intangible resources and, therefore, are identified as intellectual capital. The market value of an organization is the sum of its financial capital and intellectual capital. In turn, the intellectual capital is the summation of human capital (HC), structural capital (SC), and relational capital (RC).

### Intellectual Capital (IC)

IC are intangible resources that consists of employees' knowledge and ability, knowledge of business processes and routines, and organizations' knowledge of internal and external relationships. IC enables ambidexterity at the operational level through its three components, namely, human, structural and RC (Tarasova and Vertakova 2022).

Organizations carry out two types of simultaneous learning, namely, exploitation and exploration learning. Exploration learning entails search, discovery, variation, and experimentation, while exploitation learning focuses more on selection, refinement, efficiency, and realization or implementation. Rather than a spectrum of ambidexterity ranging from exploration to exploitation, these modes of learning coexist simultaneously, albeit through separate units of SC rather than at the opposite ends.

The three main components of IC along with the corresponding ambidextrous characteristics are:

i. HC can be understood as knowledge, abilities, or capabilities and skills utilized by individual employees. The organizationwide HC is the sum total of knowledge and organizational memory about prioritizing of various organizational issues. It comprises of the individual skills, collective experience, general know-how, and management expertise of all employees within the organizations. There are two kinds of HC, namely, specialist and generalist. Specialist HC promotes intensive training to improve domain-specific knowledge skills in the current area of work. Generalist HC encompasses extensive training to develop new set of multiple skills for prospective business requirements. It possess the ability to combine, comprehend, and apply new knowledge.

ii. SC can be understood as the organizational knowledge used through processes and systems to execute business transactions, structures, and databases for storing details of these business transactions to help employees to achieve optimal overall organizational and business performance. IC represents an accumulation of an organization's knowledge including strategies, leadership norms, intellectual property (IP) like patents, standard operating procedures (SOPs), quality, productivity, efficiency standards, organizational culture, management style, systems and processes, and networks and infrastructures that remain with the organization, even when the employees go home. Overall, SC incorporates all nonhuman knowledge resources. There are two kinds of SC, namely, mechanistic and organic. Mechanistic SC entails the conformity of the members of its organization to establish and maintain its organizational rules and social norms. Organic SC is encouraged proactively to create and shape values, norms, and culture that reinforce organizational success.

iii. RC can be understood as the knowledge embodied in connections, interactions, and, interrelationship channels, alliances, groups, communities, and networks between organizations and its customers, partners, suppliers, and employees. There are two kinds of RC, namely, cooperative and entrepreneurial. Cooperative RC comprises of dense network of connections and a shared understanding how knowledge can be shared and worked upon. It fosters the use of job-based compensations, set of norms, rules, pay structures, and procedures of monitoring and reporting. Entrepreneurial RC comprises of initiatives, flexibility, and resilience. It consists of three components, namely, mindshare, engagement, and affect. The first component highlights the significance of shared representation, meanings of shared systems and understanding among the members of an organization. The second component reflects the connections and configurations of a group of individuals within the organizations. And, the third component encompasses the expectations, motives, trust, and norms of interpersonal exchanges within the organization. Entrepreneurial RC fosters the use of target-based compensations, incentive structures, and procedures of monitoring and reporting.

## Scaling

Scaling is the characteristic defining feature of a startup aspiring to become a unicorn (Sisney 2021).

Intangible assets differ from tangible assets because they are not what an economist would term as *rivals in use*, that is consumption by one individual customer does not deduct or reduce the amount left for another. Compared to most physical assets, once an intangible asset has been created or acquired, it can be used again and again at relatively very low costs. While rivalry might be the economic primitive behind scalability, scalability can be used for convenience and conveying corresponding implications for requisites like delivery, traceability, security, fault tolerance, infrastructure, and so on.

While network effects can be found among both tangible and intangible assets, big network effects are obtainable within intangible assets only. Consequently, intangible assets are significantly more scalable than tangible assets and scalability becomes supercharged with network effects.

## IP

The management of a firm's intellectual property (IP) is a significant element of innovation strategy. If a firm's competitive advantage is at least partly based on technology, the sustainability of this advantage is critically dependent on disabling competitor's from readily imitating (termed as appropriating) its offerings, that is, products, services, or experiences. If successful, this would not only enable competitor's to compete head-on with the firm but would do so with the additional advantage of not having to recoup the investment that the firm has made while developing new technology and corresponding competencies.

IP includes a wide range of intangible assets, but in light of this book's focus, it refers to all technology-based intangible assets of the firm: an idea or a design for a new offering, a software package, or that can be protected as a property right under the legal framework that includes patents, copyrights, and trademarks. Patents are associated with technical innovations and, hence, are focal to technological innovations; copyrights are associated with various forms or manifestations of artistic expressions; and trademarks are associated with corporate or offering identity and are focal to the functions and activities of marketing (Poltorak and Lerner 2011).

Firms can benefit commercially from monetization of IPs depending upon their criticality and lifecycle of the offerings or innate technologies. The rapid growth of technology licensing, sale of patent portfolios, or securitization are clear reflection of a market for rapidly changing technologies (Halt et al. 2017). The various forms of monetization are as follows:

1. Embedding of new technologies in the offerings that are sold, leased, and rented to the target customers.
2. Employment of new technologies in the production process, which reduces the cost and/or improves the quality of the offerings that are produced and marketed.
3. Licensing of new technologies disembodied from the offerings. This also enables the variant of cross-licensing that involves companies bartering technologies through the licensing process, netting out the difference in terms of valuation.
4. Outright sale of technologies. An illustration of this is Google's acquisition of Motorola Mobility for U.S.$12.5 billion, which was simply a portfolio of 17,000 patents of Motorola Mobility. Similarly, Facebook's acquisition of around 16+ companies in the last few years primarily for obtaining the HC in the form of hard-to-get talented employees rather than their patent portfolio.
5. Securitization of the technologies (i.e., IP) whereby the buyer participates on the debt side at rates far lower than typical VC lenders while the owner continues to have equity component of the royalty stream.

6. Acquiring technologies (i.e., IP) from insolvent/failed companies or independent inventors and monetizing them by bringing infringement suits against companies whose offerings infringe on this IP. Such companies are mainly in the business of recovering damages and collecting royalties on unauthorized use of IP.

## Open Source

Open-source software is transforming the software industry and shifting the traditional build versus buy decision process (Bessen 2022). There are a growing number of open-source alternatives to traditional closed-source applications and tools. Developers will increasingly look toward such open-source packages as key free, libre, and open-source software (FLOSS) components for systems that they are designing and developing. Early FLOSS projects were focused on development tools, small components, and middleware. In many cases, these projects would create a FLOSS replacement for a piece of commercial software, matching the external specifications so that the open version could serve as a replacement for the closed one. More recently, there has been a growth in FLOSS applications, such as SugarCRM and OrangeHRM, that are built upon an open-source infrastructure. For example, SugarCRM is used with the Apache HTTP server, MySQL or PostgreSQL, and PHP.

FLOSS products have made significant inroads into companies even to support their software infrastructure. Many of the most heavily used websites, including Google and Yahoo, are built on FLOSS technologies, and the Windows operating system includes licensed open-source components.

Additional details are available in the Appendix section (**A.5.2 Open Source**) available online.

## Entrepreneurship

Entrepreneurship is not a state of being but of becoming entrepreneurial, that is, it is a process. The entrepreneurship process is characterized by proactiveness, innovativeness, and risk-taking (Passiante 2020; Hisrich and Ramadani 2017). Becoming entrepreneurial is relevant to organizations of all types (traditional or startups) and sizes (large and small enterprises); this process fundamentally involves creation of value and embracing the irreducible uncertainty that lies at the heart of all prospective business opportunities. The entrepreneurship process primarily entails discovery, evaluation, and exploitation of business opportunities on a continual basis.

The process of discovering new business opportunities involves assessment of the current products, services, or offerings in the target market and their improvement from the customer's perspective via digitalization or digital transformation. Furthermore, it involves understanding the current business model that creates and delivers value for the customer as well as considering reconfigurations of the business models for delivering additional or enhanced value for the customer. Evaluation of the business opportunities entails assessment of the potential market size for this opportunity as also their ability to deliver the necessary value of this offering based on the resources available or accessible to them including factors such as risk, finance, and others. Opportunity exploitation entails arranging for finance, resources (human, consumables, etc.), and activities (procurement, production, sales and distribution, etc.), including availability of infrastructure and facilities that are essential for successful creation and delivery of value to the customer.

## Ambidexterity

The commonalities and differences between the exploratory and exploitative areas of the business and how they link and interact are key. O'Reilly and Tushman showed that successful ambidextrous organizations had been able to set up structures that were independent enough to enable breakthrough innovation and different ways of working to emerge while connected enough at the senior level to keep them aligned to vision, strategic goals, or needs. This requires the senior teams and management to be ambidextrous in understanding the divergent needs of the different kinds of business areas, combining the ability to make difficult tradeoffs or decisions with the visionary thinking required of entrepreneurs. The concept of the *ambidextrous organization* was first described by Charles O'Reilly and Michael Tushman in their 2004 HBR article as a way to capture the challenge inherent in businesses being able to make steady improvements to existing models while still developing breakthrough innovations. This was akin to the challenge of constantly looking backward in attending to the products and processes of the past while also gazing forwards and preparing for the innovations that will define a new future (Kraner 2018).

### Strategic Innovative Entrepreneurship

New innovation strategies of strategic entrepreneurship in turbulent markets require collaboration of the personnel of different departments, presence of organizational flexibility, and also the breaking and/or changing of current routines. Strategic innovative entrepreneurship is a distinct process for bringing something new to a market, based on a combination of innovation, opportunity identification, and business growth (Passiante 2020). Hence, innovation is an essential component of strategic entrepreneurship and represents the means through which market opportunity is capitalized by firms. The various types of innovations support strategic entrepreneurship of firms with new strategies, products, processes, dynamic capabilities, or business models.

### Continuous Innovation

Innovations are the basis for the competitiveness and, hence, accelerated growth of companies. Everything starting from new promising ideas to new products and from new business concepts to industry-shaping success stories are easily labeled as innovation (Kraner 2018; Duffey 2019). In order to be referred as an innovation, it is necessary that a new idea be implemented or applied. In a product innovation, for example, it is not enough to discover penicillin, but also to develop a market-ready product. The same also applies to process innovations (e.g., introduction of the *drive-in* in 1971 or cashless payment by smartphone using near-field communication technology). Even in the case of conceptual innovations (e.g., novel organizational structures), innovation can only be considered when these have been implemented or applied.

The definitions of innovation include:

- The introduction of something new
- A new idea, method, or device
- The creation of new products or services

- The introduction of a new idea into the marketplace in the form of a new product or service or an improvement in organization or process
- A successful exploitation of new ideas
- Creating value out of new ideas, new products, new services, or new ways of doing things

All the definitions of innovation have in common the feature that innovation is a deliberate and conscious process of change toward something (for the first time) *new*. The definition used here is intended to highlight three subject areas, namely, product, process, concept innovation. All three are relevant to the economic view of innovation.

Process innovation includes changes in a production or business process. Through technical or organizational modifications, the process of service provision is changed or optimized. This makes it possible, for example, to produce products more cost-effectively, at higher quality or in less time. Increasing productivity, producing new products, or avoiding environmental damage are typical objectives of process innovation. As a historical example of a process innovation, the introduction of assembly line production in the automobile industry by Henry Ford in 1913 can be cited. With this new process, the Ford Motor Company was able to significantly increase production speed and significantly reduce unit costs.

Change or the development of a business model, a political or social concept, and the like, fall under conceptual innovations. In the 1950s and 1960s, IKEA developed a new business model, in which furniture was bought in a new way—for example, through the involvement of customers in its transport and construction. Examples of newer business models that were made possible through the Internet are WhatsApp or YouTube.

Innovation can be categorized depending on:

- Technology (e.g., radio networks)
- Product (e.g., a mobile phone)
- Service (e.g., location-based services)
- Marketing/culture (e.g., smartphone represents lifestyle)
- Organization and process (e.g., automated service procedures)
- Business model/strategy (e.g., mobile-based payments)

The nature of innovation can be described using different dimensions like:

1. Closed versus open: This dimension aims to characterize innovations in terms of the nature of interactions between the initiator of the original idea, his or her affiliation or reference group within which the idea is incubated, and the *external world*, including all relevant interest groups and individuals that are expected to contribute to or benefit from the end result of the development work.

    a. Closed innovation refers to innovation based on internal and centralized R&D and deep vertical integration of the value chain from research to commercialization. The term *closed* is also used to refer to secrecy and various formal arrangements for the protection of original ideas and all possibly useful intermediate products of the development work. This may be the case if the original idea has been evaluated to bear significant economic potential and if the endeavor is prone to an expensive failure. This may be the case for the development of new drugs.

    b. Open innovation, on the other hand, stands for innovation practices designed to take full advantage of the changing knowledge landscape (e.g., abundance of knowledge) and business environment (e.g., availability of VC and various services) through a systematic utilization of external knowledge and search for additional commercialization channels for technologies that have been developed but cannot be commercialized inhouse. The term *open* is also associated with the free exchange of ideas, the underlying assumption being that without distributing ideas, crossing borders, and seeking international cooperation, there simply is no way of achieving breakthrough innovations.

The advocates of open innovation stress the value of reciprocity: in exchange for ideas and information that one conveys to the community, he or she will be rewarded by additional ideas and information that may prove useful later. The idea of open innovation is perhaps best represented by the numerous software developer forums one can find on the Internet, and the open source software licenses (e.g., GNU GPL).

2. Incremental/continuous/sustaining versus radical/discontinuous/ disruptive: This dimension has to do with the scale and *gradient* of changes resulting from the innovation.

    a. *Incremental* and *continuous* innovation implies the idea of a foreseeable, step-by-step development process, in which particular functional or structural features of the product or service concerned are gradually enhanced or replaced by different features.

       If the innovation is sustaining, it usually allows an organization to maintain its current approach to the target market. For example, if the innovation is related to the fuel efficiency of cars, the resulting new car will probably be marketed and used in pretty much the same way as before. Fuel efficiency (i.e., km/liter) has been an important development target in the automotive industry for decades, and most new cars have always been marketed as being better in this respect—regardless of the underlying technology.

    b. A radical innovation would significantly change the supply and demand conditions in the market or product category concerned. For example, introduction of a cheap and pollution-free electric car that could replace petrol-driven cars would certainly do that. Radical innovations typically involve large leaps in understanding new ways of seeing the problem at hand, and taking bigger risks than many people involved feel comfortable about. If the innovation is radical, it usually is disruptive, in the sense that it will render erstwhile successful products and/or business models obsolete.

       Disruptive or transformative innovation refers to when the major scale of an innovation causes new markets to be created. This is also the case if the innovation drastically changes the rules of the game of a market or the behavior of the user. A good example of this is Apple's iTunes. The invention of the mp3 standard was not, in itself, a disruptive or transformative innovation, but a radical one. However, the introduction of user-friendly iPods in conjunction with iTunes profoundly changed both the market and user behavior, resulting in a disruptive innovation. As a consequence, playing, converting, buying, or organizing music, audio books, or films has been massively altered. For established providers, Apple's offering constitutes a *destructive* innovation.

3. Local/modular versus systemic/ architectural: This dimension is closely related to the scope of changes that result from or are necessary for the adoption and diffusion of the innovation.

   a. A local or modular innovation implies that the functional principles or performance of a product or its component may change, but the way it connects to other surrounding systems remains unchanged. For example, let's assume that someone develops new technology that doubles the power of mobile phone batteries. If the new batteries, based on that technology, can be designed in such a way that they do not necessitate changes in the design or manufacturing of the phones, the innovation can be called modular. Manufacturers and customers may easily change old batteries to the new ones without being forced to change their behavior in any major way—both can benefit from the development, which provides them with new options for the marketing and use of mobile phones.

   b. A systemic or architectural innovation implies that the introduction of the new technology, product, service, business model, and so on calls for changes in the structural or functional features of other related products or systems, and/or in the behavior of other actors, for example, suppliers, distributors, or customers.

## Business Model

A company's business model should support and enable it to achieve its vision and mission. A business model is closely related to the traditional business cases used in business schools. The idea of a business case is essentially constructing a story with enough detail about what the company is trying to achieve, how they will do it, for whom, when, what the costs and rewards will be, and so on. In other words, it is the story about the underlying innovative idea and how they are going to implement it (Kale 2017). A business model is the next step to assist in visualization of a business.

Business model is a framework for finding a systematic way to unlock long-term value for an organization while delivering value to customers and capturing value through monetization strategies. Business Model Canvas (BMC) is a structured and visual framework of strategy on a single page for the identification and summary of the relevant components that are essential building blocks of a business, namely, customer segments, value propositions, channels, customer relationships, revenue streams, key activities, key resources, key partnerships, and cost structure (Voigt Kai-Ingo et al. 2017).

The BMS is divided into three blocks:

1. Desirability: Desirability consists of customer segments, value propositions, channels, and customer relationships. This block places emphasis on whether there is a fit between a company's offerings and the market. A company should begin with defining the customer segments that they would like to target. Next, with the target group in mind, the company needs to define their value proposition, which is the value they are creating for their target group. With a clear picture of the target group and the company's value proposition, companies can define the channels to reach customers and the envisaged relationship between the company and the target group.

2. Feasibility: Feasibility consists of key partners, key activities, and resources. Key partners refer to companies and people who support the business, for example, suppliers, transport partners, and marketing agencies. On the other hand, key activities are related to the core processes that must be carried out to deliver value to customers. Key resources consist of manpower, equipment, and assets, which are fundamental to the functioning of the business. This block mainly identifies the required resources and helps companies perform the check on whether they have access to the right resources and partners to carry out their activities.

3. Viability: Viability consists of cost structure and revenue streams, and, essentially represents the bottom line of the business. Firstly, it is important to identify potential revenue streams which are company's source of income (e.g., sale of product, services, and advertisement spaces), and revenue models which is the strategy to manage the revenue streams (which the company can leverage on). After the selection of the appropriate and relevant revenue model(s), companies

can identify the different cost areas such as personnel, marketing, and technological. By looking at both revenue and costs, a company is able to create forecasts such as required investments, cost per acquisition, customer lifetime value, and breakeven points.

Some of the most common revenue models include:

i. Transaction-based revenue model is the most direct revenue model where companies charge a certain price for providing a service or product each time.

ii. Commission revenue model, where companies earn a commission fee instead of the full profit with each transaction. This revenue model is commonly used in online marketplaces where the companies earning the commission act as an intermediary between the buyer and seller. In this context, the commission earned by the company can be seen as a reward for helping the seller close a successful transaction. A commission revenue model can be implemented without having to offer products or services, but this also means that the revenue generated is limited and difficult to scale.

iii. Subscription-based revenue model, where instead of paying one time for the use of the products and services, customers pay for over a longer period of time, usually on a monthly or annual basis. A subscription-based model allows for companies to maintain a more regular and certain cash flow. However, for a company to be able to implement such a revenue model, its product or service needs to command a regular use demand and be sufficiently useful that users will want to use and pay for it on a regular basis.

iv. Freemium revenue model works by offering the basic features or services for free and charging for advanced features. Such a model is rising in popularity due to the ability to allow customers to try the product without a financial commitment and attracting them to pay for an important add-on later. However, this model requires effective strategization to determine what to offer such that it entices customers but not too much that customers are comfortably satisfied without paying for the premium features. For instance, iCloud provides 5 GB of storage space for free. Once users begin to rely on the storage space for various purposes, they will be enticed to pay extra to increase their capacity and to reduce the switching costs.

v. Affiliate revenue model where companies earn a commission by promoting links to other products and services on their site. The model usually works with a tracking system for the company selling the products and services to track if the successful purchase comes from an affiliate site. Commission is then paid out to the company depending on the transactions that originated from the company site. This can also be used in combination with advertisements.

## Growth Strategy

Growth is defined as an increase of sales, profits, number of employees, market share, penetration into new markets, and so on. Here, it should be noted that there is a difference between the words *growth* and *expansion*, which, very often, in daily conversations are used interchangeably. Growth is the first significant increase of sales, profits, and/or number of employees after starting the business; expansion represents a more controlled increase of market share and company's size after the growth stage (Hisrich and Ramadani 2017).

Growth of a business can be seen from several perspectives:

1. Strategic growth has to do with the changes that the company makes during the interaction with the environment as a whole. This is related with the way the company develops its ability to exploit opportunities in the market and the ways of using assets to create sustainable competitive advantage.
2. Financial growth has to do with the business growth as a commercial entity and include increase of sales, costs, and investments to achieve that sales and profits. Financial growth also includes the increase of the value of the company's assets as an important measure of its success.
3. Structural growth is related to the company's changes with regard to the organization of the internal system, in particular, managerial roles and responsibilities, reporting relationships, communication links, and resource control systems.

4. Organizational growth has to do with changes in processes, culture, and attitudes of the company. In particular, attention is given to changes that are related to the entrepreneur's role and style of leadership as the company *moves* from being a small to a large company.

Additional details are available in the Appendix section (**A.5.1 Growth Strategy**) available online.

## Conclusion

This chapter presented aspects related to strategizing for the success of the contemporary digital enterprises, namely, intangible capital, intellectual capital, intellectual property, ambidexterity, continuous innovation, innovative entrepreneurship, business model, and growth. The success of firms in the current dynamic and uncertain business environment is largely determined by the capacity of the organizations to respond to changes in the environment and to constantly work on the innovation of their strategic orientation. Valuation of a startup is critically dependent on the stupendous enhancement of the intangible capital, which majorly measures the future potential of the startup's business. The chapter ends with highlighting the most predominant aspect of a startup lifecycle, that is, continuous innovation for accelerated growth.

*This chapter presented aspects related to strategizing for the success of the contemporary digital enterprises including intangible capital, intellectual capital, ambidexterity, scaling, entrepreneurship, business model, and growth. It highlighted aspects related to unleashing the unicorn, namely, Built_to_ Innovate organization, scaling, continuous innovation, and growth.*

# CHAPTER 6

# Style

## Topics Covered

- Contemporary Software Development
  - Experimental Software Development
    - *Iterative*
    - *Empathetic*
    - *Interactive*
    - *Interpretable*
  - Rapid Prototyping
  - Domain-specific Development
  - Multiparadigm Development
  - Decentralized Multiorganizational and Multisite Dev.
- Software Evolution
- Agent-Based Development
- Learning Organization
- Nature-Inspired Solutions and Strategies
- Bias
- Safety
- Collaborative Leadership

## Introduction

*This chapter presents an overview of contemporary software development efforts characterized by customer empathy, experiments and iterations, multiparadigm, multisite and multiorganization development, and, focus on domain-specific functionalities. It introduces the current trend of utilizing nature-inspired strategies and solutions for swift computations and validations.*

# Contemporary Software Development

The software development process contains three generic phases, namely, definition, development, and maintenance (Brown 2023; Vuppalapati 2021; Lee 2013):

1. The definition phase focuses on what information is to be processed, what function and performance are desired, what interfaces are to be established, what design constraints exist, and what validation criteria are required to define a successful system. Three subphases of this phase are:
   - System analysis, defining the role of each element in a computer-based system, ultimately identifying the role software will play
   - Project analysis, defining in details software project planning, allocating resources, estimates costs, defining work tasks and schedules, setting quality plans, and identifying risks
   - Requirements analysis, defining in more detail the information domain and software function before work can begin.
2. The development phase focuses on how the software architecture and associated data structures are to be designed, how procedural details are to be implemented, how the design will be translated into a programming language, and how testing will be performed. Three subphases of this phase are:
   - Software design, translating the requirements for the software into a set of representations that describe data structure, architecture, and algorithmic procedure
   - Software coding, performing the translation from design representations into an artificial language that results in instructions executable by the computer
   - Software testing, uncovering defects in function, in logic, and in implementation.
3. The evolution phase focuses on changes that are associated with error corrections, adaptations required as the software's environment evolves, and modifications due to enhancements brought about by changing customer requirements. The evolution phase reapplies the

steps of the definition and development phases but does so in the context of pre-existing software.

## Experimental Software Development

An experiment is an investigation of a testable hypothesis where one or more *independent* variables are manipulated to measure their effect on one or more *dependent* variables. Each combination of values of the independent variables is an *observation set* (ObSet) (Luca and Bazerman 2020; Felderer and Travasos 2020; Shull et al. 2008). Controlled experiments allow to determine:

- How the variables are related
- Whether a cause–effect relationship exists between them

The simplest experiments have just two ObSet representing two levels of a single independent variable (e.g., using a tool versus not using a tool). More complex experimental designs arise when there are more than two levels or more than one independent variable is used.

Additional developments are available in the Appendix section (**A.6.1 Experimental Software Development**) available online.

## Rapid Prototyping

Rapid prototyping covers all activities that result in a prototype that is an easily modifiable and extensible working model of a proposed system—though not necessarily representative of a complete system—which provides later users of the application with a physical representation of key parts of the system before implementation (Liou 2008).

The prototyping-oriented software development strategy is quite similar to the standard waterfall development strategy, but the requirements analysis and the requirements definition phases overlap considerably, and design, implementation, and testing phases overlap together a great deal. The phases rather than distinct stages become more of activities within a continuous process of development (Stackowiak and Kelly 2020). Figure 6.1 shows a comparison of the waterfall and prototyping-oriented software development lifecycle.

(a)

(b)

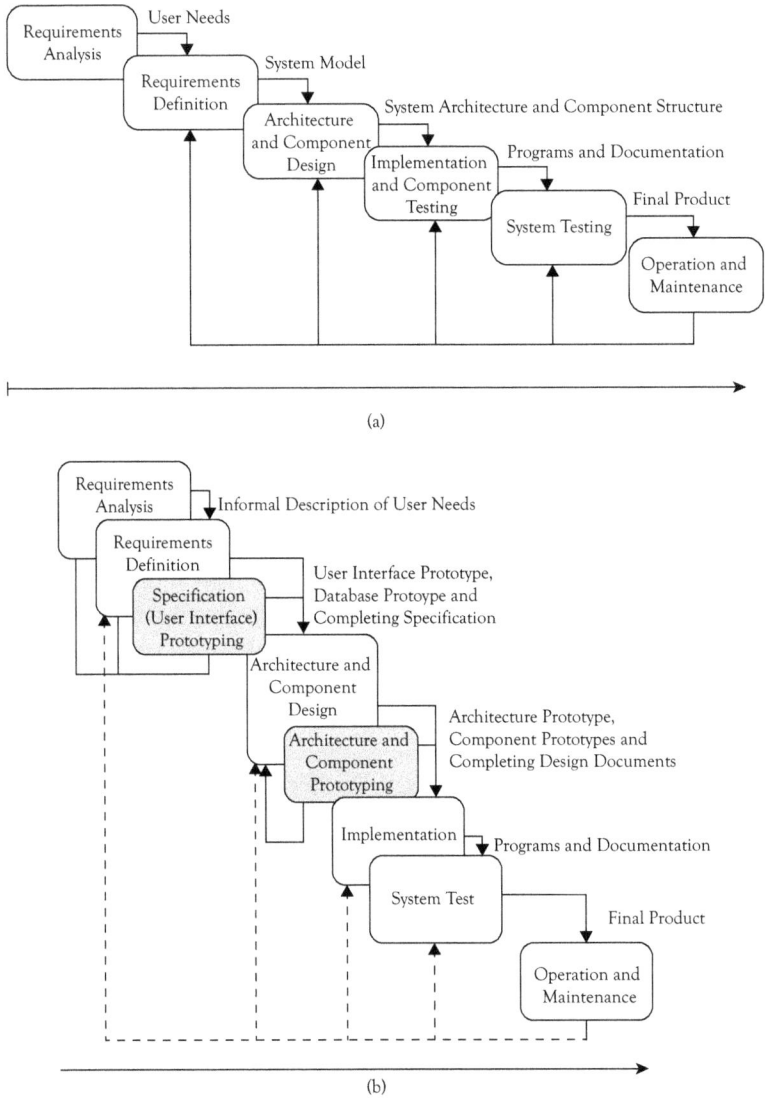

*Figure 6.1  Software development lifecycle: (a) Waterfall and (b) Prototyping-oriented*

The iterative development process is as follows:

i. Based on a rough requirements analysis, the description of user needs is prepared.

ii. Based on the user's needs, with tool support, a prototype of the external behavior is produced.

iii. Based on the prototype, experiments are carried out that reflect real application conditions to evaluate whether the user's requirements have been met.

iv. If the user requirements are met, terminate, else go back to ii.

The production of a prototype is an iterative process. Thus, a pseudo-lifecycle is introduced within the development lifecycle through a *pseudo-implementation* as early as possible. This pseudo-lifecycle is terminated when the later user and the developer agree on the system model (prototype).

The overlapping of the individual activities (see Figure 6.1) and the type of intermediate results—executable prototypes rather than mere static descriptions—reduces the risk of making a specification error or a design error. The learning effect achieved by experimenting with the phase results (prototypes) opens a new dimension with respect to quality assurance.

This highlights the significant difference between the two approaches. The goals of any software lifecycle are:

- Reduction of risk
- Successful quality assurance
- Exploitation of the learning effect of experimenting under real conditions

According to the waterfall software lifecycle, implementation occurs as late as possible and only after all the details of the requirements definition and design processes have been clarified. The application of the prototyping-oriented software lifecycle promotes the implementation of a prototype as early as possible. This is done because the preceding goals are more readily achieved if the requirements definition and the system architecture are developed incrementally on the basis of a progressively tested model. The purpose of this model is to permit the ongoing affirmation of the dynamic behavior of the system.

### Domain-Specific Development

Throughout the history of software development, developers have always sought to improve productivity by improving abstraction. Domain-specific modeling (DSM) provides a way to continue to raise the description of software to more abstract levels. These higher abstractions are based not on current coding concepts or on general-purpose concepts but on concepts that are specific to each application domain (Bjorner 2021; Reinhartz-Berger et al. 2013).

A domain is defined as an area of interest for a particular development effort. Domains can be a:

- Horizontal, technical domain, such as persistency, user interface, communication, or transactions.
- Vertical, functional, business domain, such as telecommunication, banking, robot control, insurance, or retail.

A higher level of abstraction generally leads to better productivity. This covers not only the time and resources needed to make the product in the first place but also its maintenance. Domain-specific approaches are reported to be on average 300 to 1,000 percent more productive than general-purpose modeling languages or manual coding practices. Such productivity increase is usually so significant that companies do not want to make their DSM solution public as it becomes critical to their competitive advantage. This is especially true for vertical DSM solutions. They are also inherently less known because their domains are narrower and the applicable practitioner community is smaller.

Thus, a DSM has the following characteristics:

- DSM fundamentally raises the level of abstraction, while at the same time, narrowing down the design space, often to a singular range of products for a particular company.
- DSM obviates the need to make error-prone mappings from domain concepts to design concepts and on to programming language concepts.

- DSM language solves the problem only once by visually modeling the solution using only familiar domain concepts. The final products are then automatically generated from these high-level specifications with domain-specific code generators.

## Multiparadigm Development

The central idea of Thomas Kuhn's extraordinarily influential book *The Structure of Scientific Revolutions* is that the development of science in normal periods of science is driven by adherence to what Kuhn called a paradigm. Paradigm refers to a constellation of shared beliefs, values, instruments and techniques, and even metaphysics that functions as a context or frame-of-reference for the normal activities of science: questions, solutions, experimental data, interpretations, and so on. Analogously, in the context of computer science and information systems, paradigm refers to the constellation of subdisciplines with their own set of beliefs, values, axioms and principles, models, methods, and methodologies (Carreira et al. 2020).

The engineering process of system under study (SUS) requires numerous distinct disciplines to be employed. Each discipline typically creates a design (also said to be a view or understanding) of the system for its own purposes in the form of a model. A model of a system is an abstraction (a representation) to make predictions or inferences about a select reality. Models are created using abstractions, heuristics of decomposition, and tools of analysis typical of each discipline. Different models are expressed precisely and unambiguously using correspondingly different modeling formalisms like differential equations, finite-state automata, state charts, Petri nets, among others. Distinct formalisms exist because they are more concise and enable answering efficiently to distinct classes of questions. Indeed, no single formalism can be used to model all aspects of a system, as the formalism to be used depends on the nature of the problem to be solved. Models expressed at distinct levels of abstraction are linked to one another through structure-preserving maps. Indeed, an overarching issue with distinct formalisms is merging models of the same system through these maps.

Multiparadigm modeling (MPM) has been recognized as a powerful approach (a paradigm in its own right) that may be helpful in designing, as well as communicating and reasoning about SUS, which are notoriously complex because of their cross-discipline borders and interdomain interactions. The application of MPM requires modeling everything explicitly, using the most appropriate formalism(s), at the most appropriate level(s) of abstraction. This suggests that a paradigm can be understood as an arrangement of the properties in each of the dimensions described earlier: the formalisms and the levels of abstraction in the modeling activities.

During the course of system development, to tackle complexity, three basic abstraction approaches are commonly combined:

i. Model abstraction (and its dual, refinement) is used when focusing on a particular set of properties of interest.

ii. Architectural decomposition (and its dual, component composition) is used when the problem can be broken into parts, each with an appropriate interface.

iii. View decomposition (and its dual, view merge) is used to enable the collaboration between multiple stakeholders, each with different concerns. Each viewpoint allows the evaluation of a stakeholder-specific set of properties.

It can be said that an MPM framework aims to support (meta-)tool builders who assist practitioners to reason about SUS and figure out which formalisms, abstractions, workflows, and supporting methods, techniques, and tools are most appropriate to carry out their task(s).

Oftentimes, formalisms are general-purpose, and hard to use by modelers (domain users, or domain experts) who need to start by picking the most adequate formalism based on its well-known semantics, for example, Petri nets for workflows and concurrency, or Statecharts for describing event-based systems, among others. However, having to master mathematical notation poses a steep learning curve. To alleviate this problem, specialized languages, called DSM languages, are created to simplify the act of expressing the modeler's specification intent. The constructs in these languages are designed to be closer to the way domain experts are used to conceptualize problems.

### *Decentralized Multiorganizational, Multisite Development*

A distributed system can be centralized or decentralized. In a centralized distributed system, the master node is responsible for breaking down computational tasks and data to distribute the load across the network. While as in a decentralized distributed system, there is no master node, every node is autonomous to distribute the computational load across the network.

Most companies are unaware of the huge collective competitive advantages or network power available in the alliance networks and are instead preoccupied with capitalizing on the advantages gained from singular alliances, one alliance at a time. Alliances (or partnerships or joint ventures) are important tools for building and reinforcing the collective competitive advantage or network power. A company's network power is simply not a summation of the network advantages resulting from individual alliances in isolation. Alliances can be defined as enduring and formalized collaborative relationships between two or more firms that involve significant exchanges of information, resources, and influence or decision power; alliance networks are conduits across which information, resources, and decisions flow, reflecting the company's network power (NP) (see Chapter 8 subsection *Network of Projects*).

With the advancement in computing technologies, including cloud computing, distributed computing, blockchain, and the Internet of Things (IoT), the existing frameworks and management approaches do not apply satisfactorily. This has given rise to the requirement for software to be scalable, sustainable, and suitable for distributed computing environments. In turn, this suggests a requirement for management methods with evolutionary lifecycles and software development approaches that take into account distributed working practices and distributed team management working in virtual operating environments (see Chapter 9 section "Team Based Management").

## Software Evolution

Due to the rapid development of computer hardware and software, the demands and costs of software changes are increasing continuously.

From the day that a large software system goes into service, functional, performance, operational, and environmental requirements change constantly. Software changes comprise a major portion of software lifecycle costs. Because software changes are needed so frequently and continuously, it is best described as software evolution (Furrer 2019; Johnson et al. 2005).

Successful software evolves inevitably, but the process of evolution leads to degraded structure and increasing complexity. Changes include fixing errors, adding enhancements, and making optimizations. Besides the problems whose solutions required the changes in the first place, the implementation of the changes themselves generated and added their own problems. Hence, mechanisms have to be developed for evaluating, controlling, and making changes.

Software has to evolve to correct faults, to improve performance or other attributes, or to adapt to the changed environment. Accordingly, software evolution can be of four types:

1. Corrective corresponds to the faulty implementation or incomplete testing or defective specification.
2. Adaptive corresponds to inevitable evolution in the contextual environment on account of changing regulations, standards, or technology.
3. Perfective corresponds to inevitable evolution in the customer or user requirements.
4. Preventive corresponds to inevitable evolution necessitated by anticipated evolution in the requirement specifications, customer or user requirements, or even environmental conditions.

Consequently, software evolution must be considered at each stage of the software development or engineering process:

- During the requirements stage, areas of future enhancement and potential revision should be noted, software portability issues discussed, and system interfaces that might impact software maintenance considered.

- During the design stage, data design, architecture design, and procedural design should be evaluated for ease of modification, modularity, and functional independence.
- During the coding stage, suitability of style and standards of coding and internal documentation should be stressed.

At every stage, software evolution is dependent of inherent characteristics of the following:

i. Complexity: an operating measure of a software system's aggregation and distribution of components/complexes
ii. Modularity: an operating measure of the extent to which a system can be broken down into small independent building blocks
iii. Flexibility: an operating measure of a software system's independence from any specific resulting application
iv. Portability: an operating measure of a software system's independence from its technical environment

## Agent-Based Development

An agent-based system may contain one or more agents. There are cases in which a single-agent solution is appropriate. However, the multiagent case—where the system is designed and implemented as several interacting agents—is arguably more widespread and more interesting from a software engineering standpoint (Poole and Macworth 2017). Multiagent systems (MAS) can be defined as a collection of possibly heterogeneous computational agents, each with their own problem-solving capabilities and which are able to interact in order to reach an overall goal. MAS are ideally suited to representing problems that have multiple problem-solving methods, multiple perspectives, and/or multiple problem-solving entities. Such systems have the traditional advantages of distributed and concurrent problem solving but have the additional advantage of sophisticated patterns of interaction (Shehory and Sturm 2014; Cao 2015).

Examples of common types of interactions include the following:

- Coordination (working together toward a common aim)
- Cooperation (organizing problem-solving activities so that harmful interactions are avoided or beneficial interactions are exploited)
- Collaboration (coming to an agreement that is acceptable to all parties involved)

If a problem domain is particularly complex, large, or unpredictable, the only way it can reasonably be addressed is to develop a number of functionally specific and modular agents that are specialized at solving a particular problem aspect. In MAS, applications are designed and developed in terms of autonomous software agents that can flexibly achieve their objectives by interacting with one another in terms of high-level protocols and languages.

## Learning Organization

LOs create, acquire, and transfer knowledge, and modify its behavior to reflect new knowledge and insights (Argote 2013). All organizations are LOs to some degree; though all organizations are not equally effective LOs (Banasiewicz 2021).

All organizations need to:

- Cope with rapid and unexpected changes
- Provide flexibility to cope with dynamically changing situations
- Allow frontline staff to respond with initiative based on customer needs rather than being constrained by the inertia of the traditional business processes

As companies have come to realize that their employees are their most important resource, they have recognized the need for constant behavioral change based on new learning or experiences (Dohn 2018; Wellman 2009). As organizations learn through individuals acting as agents for the company, the progress of the organization is fundamentally bound to the capability of all of its employees to change their behavior in the workplace and that too rapidly.

The only real and sustainable competitive advantage organizations have is the rate at which the organizations can learn faster than the competition via its employees.

## Nature-Inspired Solutions and Strategies

The biodiversity on Earth holds a wealth of natural strategies that may provide tailored solutions to the managerial, physical, social, economic, and environmental challenges the world faces—a practice often referred to as biomimicry, biomimetics, or bioinspiration (Primrose 2020). Despite the great potential and increasing popularity of bioinspiration as a research approach, deciding which biological systems to explore remains a challenging and complex task. For many biological systems, different strategies, morphologies and/or behaviors have evolved in response to similar functional demands—a concept known as convergent evolution. Not only does the incompleteness of the knowledge about biodiversity inhibit the identification of suitable biological strategies, but also practitioners in the field of bioinspiration often rely on the assumption that natural structures are the result of evolutionary processes that strive for optimization, thereby failing to acknowledge that these very same processes may also constrain adaptive evolution.

In recent years, there has been significant interest in the fields of bioinspired solutions and biomimetics. Bioinspired design involves the use of scientific and engineering principles in the design of engineering components and structures that are inspired by biological systems. Airfoils and aircraft wings are examples of bioinspired design that are inspired by bird flight but guided by the principles of lift and drag from aerodynamics. By contrast, biomimetics involves the design of engineering components and structures that copy biological systems. The early idea of an airplane with flapping wings is an example of biomimetics, which is based on the simple idea of copying nature without thinking carefully about the underlying scientific principles that enable such natural systems to function in the way that they do.

Aircraft, as known now, bear very little resemblance to birds. Flight was *inspired* by nature, but hundreds of years were spent trying to copy nature, with little success. The pectoral muscles of a bird occupy more than two-thirds of its whole muscular strength, whereas in man, the muscles that could operate upon attached wings would probably not exceed one-tenth of his whole mass.

Inspiration is vital—otherwise man would never have attempted to fly. But direct mimicry is the wrong direction. Similarly, computing systems may benefit much by being *inspired* by biology but should not attempt to copy biology slavishly.

The primary considerations of traditional hard computing are precision, certainty, and rigor. The traditional hard computing deals with precise computation. The rules of hard computing are strict and binding; as inputs, outputs, and procedures are all clearly defined, it generates the same precise answers without any degree of uncertainty—every time that the procedure is applied. Unless the rules or procedures are changed, the output result would never change.

By contrast, the principal notion in soft computing is that precision and certainty carry a cost, and that computation, reasoning, and decision making should exploit (wherever possible) the tolerance for imprecision, uncertainty, approximate reasoning, and partial truth for obtaining low-cost solutions (Ghaboussi 2018). The corresponding facility in humans leads to the remarkable human ability to understand distorted speech, deciphering sloppy handwriting, comprehending the nuances of natural language, summarizing text, recognizing and classifying images, driving a vehicle in dense traffic, and, more generally, making rational decisions in an environment of uncertainty and imprecision. The challenge, then, is to exploit the tolerance for imprecision by devising methods of computation that lead to an acceptable solution at low cost.

Soft computing is a consortium of methodologies that works synergistically and provides, in one form or another, flexible information processing capability for handling real-life ambiguous situations. Its aim is to exploit the tolerance for imprecision, uncertainty, approximate reasoning, and partial truth in order to achieve tractability, robustness, and low-cost solutions. The guiding principle is to devise methods of computation that lead to an acceptable solution at low cost, by seeking for an approximate solution to an imprecisely or precisely formulated problem.

# Bias

One of the unintended consequences of artificial intelligence (AI) and machine learning (ML) is the risk of making biased decisions that can lead to unfair outcomes (Albert et al. 2022). The biases can stem from the historical and societal biases in the data that is used for training the models or introduced in the model development process itself. Biased models and decisions can lead to unintended consequences such as disparity or lack of access to the issuance of credit and insurance policies for minority groups. One of the promises of AI and machine learning is to reduce bias and unfairness in financial decision making, facilitated through automation. However, despite the promise, we do not need to look far to find examples where AI and machine learning reinforced bias and amplified unfairness in decision making: from prioritizing job applications based on gender, to computer vision that discriminates based on race, to credit limit approvals that are gender biased.

When the dataset used for model development includes historically biased outcomes, the same biased dataset is then used to train potentially biased models. In AI and machine learning, the issues that lead to bias increase the risk of unfair decisions and are made worse when characteristics or features that are correlated to protected variables are used (Roberts and Tonna 2022). Protected variables are variables with legal or ethical restrictions. These can include groups that cannot be discriminated against in certain jurisdictions (e.g., demographic variables like gender and race). The models and business rules may also introduce bias.

Responsible AI means that AI systems should be designed and implemented in ways that recognize and are sensitive to human interaction contexts without infringing on core values and human rights. Responsible AI means that design, development, and use of AI must take into account societal values and moral and ethical considerations, weigh the respective priorities of values held by different stakeholders in different multicultural contexts, explain its reasoning and guarantee transparency (Agarwal and Mishra 2021).

Responsible AI is constituted of aspects like:

- Fair AI
- Explainable AI
- Accountable AI

## Safety

AI designers have already begun to develop sophisticated systems that mimic, and even surpass, human intelligence. Such advancements are capable of learning, interacting with their surroundings, and when faced with highly variable situations, making novel decisions—all in an autonomous manner. A few examples of technologies that already use AI processes are smart home devices, big data analysis software, self-driving vehicles, and health care robots, and so on. As the range of abilities of intelligent agents widens and as the breadth of functional capacity grows, it becomes imperative that designers take steps to design systems that will not act dangerously or undermine stakeholder interests (Kaneko and Yoshioka 2022; Huang, Jin, and Ruan 2023).

Because of the level of intelligence the agents possess, their increasing ability to receive information about their environment, decide, and act raises the obvious question: if something goes wrong, who is really responsible? Who has the responsibility to recover and rectify?

Even if international command and control mechanisms and regulations are put into practice to ensure the safe and consistent behavior of agent, multiagent and human–agent-level systems, ethical issues associated with their design and implementation are still likely to remain complex and intractable, with additional issues emerging along the way that will implicate or challenge a broad range of values, moral issues, and ethical principles. All these aspects and issues will have to be addressed before the systems are rolled out to the user community.

Paradoxically, when designing a self-driving vehicle, instead of the behaviors one would anticipate—a vehicle with strict, precise measures to drive in a calculated manner based on road rules, designers may choose to impart it with human-like driving behaviors. Though initial planning stages may have designers agree that safety is of utmost importance, real-world experimentation may yield results that argue in favor of self-driving vehicles responding to and behaving as if a real human driver were manning it!

## Collaborative Leadership

George Siemens, who coined the term connectionism, viewed behaviorism, cognitivism, and constructivism as pre-Internet learning theories. They all have a central premise that knowledge and learning are internal, individualistic studies (Kelly 2019). On the other hand, connectionism promotes the idea that knowledge is distributed across a network of connections, which is based on rapidly altering foundations. Connectionism is a solution that addresses the 21st-century occurrence of chaos, displaced networks, complexity, self-organizing theories, and nonhuman storage of knowledge and intelligence (Whitehead and Peckham 2022).

Here are the core principles of connectionism:

1. Learning and knowledge rests in diversity of opinions.
2. Learning is a process of connecting specialized nodes or information sources.
3. Learning may reside in nonhuman appliances.
4. Learning is ability to see connections between fields, ideas, and concepts is a core skill.
5. Nurturing and maintaining connections is needed to facilitate continual learning.
6. Capacity to know more is more critical than what is currently known.
7. Currency (accurate, up-to-date knowledge) is the intent of all connectivist learning activities.
8. Decision making is itself a learning process. Choosing what to learn and the meaning of incoming information is seen through the lens of a shifting reality. While there is a right answer now, it may be wrong tomorrow due to alterations in the information context affecting the decision.

Additional details are available in the Appendix section (**A.6.2 Collaborative Leadership**) available online.

## Conclusion

This chapter presented an overview of contemporary software development efforts characterized by customer empathy, experiments, and iterations. Contemporary software reflects the empathies of customers and end-users, and its development is typically characterized by iterations, interactions, and ability for furnishing interpretations or explanations for the outcomes of the software experiments. Consequently, the underlying preference for human-centric information systems and decision-support systems incline intelligent systems to emulate human cognition abilities resulting in an unavoidable focus on leveraging the cognitive advantage. Intelligent software development not only implies software application but also data employed for training of the models; one of the promises of AI and machine learning is to reduce bias and unfairness in financial decision making, facilitated through automation.

Codevelopment with partners networks necessitates enablement for multiparadigm, multisite and, most importantly, multiorganizational development and testing of intelligent systems. It also introduced the current trend of utilizing nature-inspired strategies and solutions for rapid computations and validations. Leadership styles typically reflect the realities of the corresponding industrial revolution. The chapter ended with an overview of the leadership styles across the four industrial revolutions.

*This chapter presented an overview of contemporary software development efforts characterized by customer empathy, experiments and iterations, multiparadigm, multisite, and multiorganization development, and, focus on domain-specific functionalities. It introduced the current trend of utilizing nature-inspired strategies and solutions for swift computations and validations.*

# CHAPTER 7

# Stuff

## Topics Covered

- Digital Products to Services to Experiences
- Products
  - Product Lifecycle (PLC)
    - *Product Design Attributes*
    - *Product Design Approaches*
  - PLC, PLM, Product Supply Chain Management (SCM) and Bill of Materials (BOM)
- Services
  - Characteristics of Services
    - *Challenges Posed by Services*
  - Classification of Services
  - SLC, SLM Service Supply Chain Management (SCM) and Bill of Processes (BOProc)
- Experiences
  - Characteristics of Experiences
    - Augmented Reality (AR) and Virtual Reality (VR)
  - Classification of Experiences
  - ELC, ELM, Experience Supply Chain Management (SCM) and Bill of Projects (BOProj)
- TRIZ, or the Theory of Inventive Problem Solving

## Introduction

*This chapter presents an overview of the products, services, and experiences forming the core offerings provided by the startup. While introducing augmented reality (AR) and virtual reality (VR) solutions, it highlights that products can be mass produced for customers. Services can be mass customized for customer preferences and experiences can be mass innovated for customer preferences.*

## From Digital Products to Services to Experiences

By the middle of the last century, the products, goods, and property came to increasingly mean an individual's exclusive right to possess, use, and, most importantly, dispose as he/she wished in the market. By 1980s, the production of goods had been eclipsed by the performance of services. These are economic activities that are not products or construction, but are transitory, are consumed at the time they are produced (and, thus, cannot be inventoried), and primarily provide intangible value. In a service economy, it is the time that is being commoditized, not prices or places or things—this also leads to a transition from Profit and Loss (P&L) to market cap as the base metric of success; what the customer is really purchasing is the access for use rather than ownership of a material good. Since the 1990s, goods are becoming more information-intensive, interactive, and are continually upgraded, and, are essentially evolving into services. Products are rapidly being equated as cost of doing business rather than as sales items; they are becoming more in the nature of *containers* or *platforms* for all sorts of upgrades and value-added services (Stark 2022). Giving away products is increasingly being used as a marketing strategy to capture the attention of the potential customers via the product *experience*. But with the advent of electronic commerce, feedback, and workflow mechanisms, services are being further transformed into multifaceted relationships between the service providers and customers, and technology is becoming more of a medium of relationships.

However, in the servicized economy, defined by shortened product lifecycles (PLC) and an ever-expanding flow of competitive goods and services, it is the customer attention (engaged through the product *experience*) rather than the resources that is becoming scarce.

## Products

### PLC

The PLC is used to map the life span of a product. There are generally four stages in the life of a product. These four stages are the introduction stage, the growth stage, the maturity stage, and the decline stage (Cantamessa and Montagna 2023). There is no set time period for the

PLC, and the length of each stage may vary. One product's entire lifecycle could be over in a few months; another product could last for years. Also, the introduction stage may last much longer than the growth stage and vice versa. Figure 7.1 also illustrates the four stages of the PLC:

1. Introduction: The introduction stage is probably the most important stage in the PLC. In fact, most products that fail do so in the introduction stage. This is the stage in which the product is initially promoted; public awareness is very important to the success of a product. If people don't know about the product, they won't go out and buy it.
2. Growth: The growth stage is where your product starts to grow. In this stage, a very large amount of money is spent on advertising. You want to concentrate on telling the consumer how much better your product is than your competitors' products.
3. Maturity: The third stage in the PLC is the maturity stage. If your product completes the introduction and growth stages, then it will spend a great deal of time in the maturity stage. During this stage, sales grow at a very fast rate and then gradually begin to stabilize. The key to surviving this stage is differentiating your product from the similar products offered by your competitors.

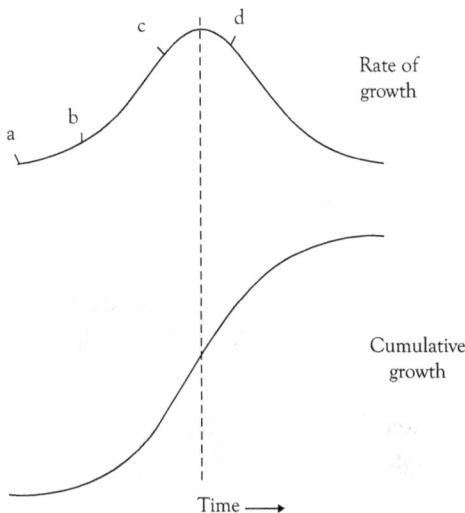

*Figure 7.1 S-curve and the PLC*

4. Decline: This is the stage in which sales of your product begin to fall. Either everyone that wants to has bought your product or new more innovative products have been created that replace yours. Many companies decide to withdraw their products from the market due to the downturn: the only way to increase sales during this period is to cut your costs and reduce your spending.

---

1. Very few products follow the same lifecycle. Many products may not even make it through all four stages; some products may even bypass stages. For example, one product may go straight from the introduction stage to the maturity stage. This is the problem with the PLC—there is no set way for a product to grow. Therefore, every product requires a great deal of research and close supervision throughout its life; without proper research and supervision, your product will probably never get out of the first stage.

2. Apart from the introduction phase, the PLC also needs to add the product development and disposal phases. In the product development phase, product variants are generated to fulfill anticipated market requirements, but at the same time, preventive measures (often on the product architecture level) must be taken to avoid excessive variety generation in later stages of PLC. During the market phase, further variants are generated (to address perceived market demand) while the preventive actions on the architectural level are enforced (to avoid excessive variety). The need for eliminating low-performing variants rises as variety proliferates and efficiently handling the growing portfolio becomes an important success factor.

---

Additional details are available in the Appendix section (**A.7.1 Product Design Attributes and Methods**) available online.

### PLC, PLM, *Product Supply Chain Management, and Bill of Materials*

The central purpose of every company must be to generate value and to improve its current competitive position. For a particular industry, these objectives are closely related to developing, producing, and selling innovative products. With the advancement of IT, novel capabilities of software-based product development and manufacturing were set into motion. These support programs integrate all necessary steps within the lifecycle of a product and thus generate a holistic approach to new development processes. This enables a company to create products with an increased product-to-market fit, improved quality, and a shorter time-to-market period. Consequently, this approach results in an improved competitive positioning for the company (Stark 2015).

PLC is a complex network with large supply chains from multiple organizations. Lifecycle assessment of products of organizations with globally dispersed manufacturing, supply chains, and international market involves various spatial and temporal constraints.

Product lifecycle management (PLM) is the business activity of managing, in the most effective way, a company's products all the way across their lifecycles; from the very first idea for a product all the way through until it is terminated or replaced.

Additional details are available in the Appendix section (**A.7.2 Product Lifecycle Management (PLM)**) available online.

Product supply chain management (SCM) involves a consistent flow of exact, timely useful information regarding basic materials, processes, and partnerships.

Bill of materials (BOM) is the basis for MRP and work schedules and describes how the product is created from assemblies and components (Roser 2017; Rissen 2019).

> This subsection discusses product-related details elaborately because similar details are applicable for services and experiences below. However, BOM gets mapped onto bill of processes (BOProc) for services and bill of projects (BOProj) for experiences respectively.

## Service

Services represent a type of relationship-based interactions (activities) between at least one service provider and one service consumer to achieve a certain service goal or solution objective. The interaction between the service provider and service consumer can happen real-time online or offline.

## Characteristics of Services

There are five differences between products and services (Annarelli et al. 2019):

i. Intangibility: Services are intangible; products such as cars, TVs, computers, clothing, and food items can be seen and touched and can be used or consumed. Most services provide some personal value to the customers. The value may be in the form of satisfaction after watching a movie, seeing a doctor for an illness, eating at a restaurant, or listening to a live concert.

ii. Perishability: Services are perishable; products can be produced ahead of time, stored, and then sold later to the customers. Perishability of services is one of the biggest challenges in managing capacity and demand for services. Empty seats in an airline have no value once the plane takes off, cricket game tickets are worthless after the game is over, and today's movie tickets are worthless tomorrow!

iii. Proximity: Most services require closer proximity of the service provider and its customers. Products can be produced anywhere in the world and shipped over long distances to the customers.

iv. Inseparability: Most services are created and consumed at the same time; in other words, there is direct consumer interaction during service. On the other hand, consumer presence is not required when producing products. Inventory of finished goods separates the producer and customer. For example, you do not have to be present when your car is manufactured at the plant.

v. Variability: Most service providers provide the same service to several customers in exactly the same way. As services invariably involve interaction between the provider and the consumer, the provider's physical and psychological condition play an important role in service delivery, and these conditions may not always be the same every day; even customers may have different perceptions of what they have received and, therefore, experience different levels of satisfaction. Moreover, the same person performing the same service may not deliver the exact same service at every performance.

## Challenges Posed by Services

The unique characteristics of services—intangibility, perishability, proximity, and simultaneity—have posed special challenges in designing and controlling service systems (Robson 2013).

1. Servicized Products or Productized Services: All the products customers buy cannot be classified strictly as goods or services. Many are in fact a combination of goods and services. For example, many Americans buy their smartphones and the wireless *service* as a bundle from AT&T, Verizon, Sprint, and other companies. Even though retail stores are classified as services, customers buy mostly goods at the supermarkets and department stores.

2. Cocreation: Introduction of self-service at gas stations, retail stores, airports, and other locations has resulted in customers interacting more actively with their services. For example, in the past, store clerks checked out the grocery items, completed the cash/credit card transactions, and bagged the items. Now, customers do all the work at *self-check* lanes. Instead of four checkout clerks working at four checkout lanes, one clerk now supervises four *self-check* lanes. The same thing is true when customers make online airline reservations or check in at the airport kiosks.

3. Service Quality: Because services are intangible and require customer interaction, it is difficult to measure the quality of service (QoS) while designing service systems. Moreover, customer satisfaction, which is a key component of service quality, is subjective and is difficult to measure. It is easier to assess product quality, while designing a manufacturing process. Variability in service outcomes also makes control and assurance of quality difficult. Finally, variability makes measurement of productivity a challenging task for managers of service organizations.

4. Service Demand and Capacity Management: While designing the capacity of manufacturing systems, inventory is used as a buffer to

account for the variability in customer demand and supply. However, perishability (no inventory) and simultaneity (direct customer interaction) make capacity management very difficult in service systems. Tools, such as *revenue management*, are specifically designed to address this challenge.

Automation and advances in digital technology have blurred some of the differences between goods and services. In the past, customers had to go physically to a bank, during normal business hours, to complete their financial transactions. With the introduction of ATMs, the customers could do their transactions at select locations any time. Then came online banking, which the customers can use to complete their bank transactions 24/7 from home. Thus, *proximity* is no longer a difference. However, direct customer interaction (simultaneity) is still valid; the interaction is now between the customers and the bank's *surrogates*—ATMs and the bank's computers.

## Types of Services

Services can also be classified based on their operational characteristics. The service process matrix classifies services based on the degree of labor intensity (high or low) versus customer interaction (high or low) for customization decisions. *Capital-intensive* services fall under low labor intensity (Quadrants I and II), while *labor-intensive* services fall under Quadrants III and IV in Figure 7.2. Customer interaction refers to the ability of the customer to personalize the services to his or her needs. In general, customization increases the cost of service.

| | | Customer interaction | |
| | | Low | High |
|---|---|---|---|
| Labor intensity | Low | Service factory (I) | Service shop (II) |
| | High | Mass service (III) | Professional service (III) |

*Figure 7.2 Service vs. interaction matrix*

The service versus interaction matrix helps companies learn the best practices of other companies, whose services have similar operational characteristics. For example, American Airlines pioneered the revenue management techniques to reduce empty seats due to *No-shows* in order to increase its revenue. Other companies in the transportation sector (airlines and trains) quickly followed the revenue management strategies. The hotel industry, which belongs to the *recreation and leisure* sector, realized that it too has similar problems—empty rooms due to no-shows (Quadrant I in Figure 7.2). Hence, they also began to apply the same revenue management strategies in hotel reservations to increase revenues.

Service factory represents services that are capital-intensive, but low in customer interaction where most customers receive the same service with very little customization—they are more like factory assembly lines. Examples of *service factory* type of services are the following:

- Airlines, trains, and buses
- Amusement parks
- Hotels
- Car rental agencies
- Mass transit in major cities

Service shop represents services that are capital-intensive, but they provide individualized customer service. Examples of *service shop* type of services are the following:

i. Hospitals
ii. Auto repair shops
iii. X-ray and MRI services

Mass service refers to labor-intensive services that provide uniform or undifferentiated services. Examples of mass service type of services include the following:

- Colleges, schools, and universities
- Retailers

- Wholesalers
- Professional sports teams

Professional services represents customized services provided by highly trained specialists. Examples of professional service type of services include the following:

- Lawyers
- Architects
- Accountants
- Engineers

### SLC, SLM, Service SCM, and BOProc

Service lifecycle (SLC) is a complex network with large supply chains from multiple organizations. Lifecycle assessment of services of organizations with globally dispersed manufacturing, supply chains, and international market involves various spatial and temporal constraints.

Service lifecycle management (SLM) is the business activity of managing, in the most effective way, a company's services all the way across their lifecycles; from the very first idea for a service all the way through until it is terminated or replaced.

Service SCM involves a consistent flow of exact, timely useful information regarding basic processes, products, and partnerships.

BOProc is the basis for services process execution and work schedules, and describes how service is created from subprocesses and products recursively.

## Experiences

With the advent of the experience economy, customer needs have shifted remarkably. Impactful customer experiences have now become a part of customer expectations. This change in customer sentiment implies a need for all companies to discover new ways of engaging with their customers (Suwelack et al. 2022). Companies that are able to recognize this shift and adapt in time, as a result of providing strong engaging experiences, will be able to benefit from the positive effects of higher perceived value, satisfaction, loyalty, word of mouth, and revenue growth.

Experience can be defined as the overall perception of a company's offering, including cognitive, emotional, physical, sensorial, spiritual, and social responses to interactions throughout the engagement with the offering (Dewey 1934; Belleghem 2015). Correspondingly, this overall perception of the offering itself is reframed as the experience offering.

In the earlier stages of the economic development, the production of products was more or less related to needs. The consumers wanted commodities, goods, and services to satisfy their needs for survival—which the manufacturing sector provided; later, the need expanded to the need for materialism, knowledge and solving problems—which the service sector provided. Customers are now looking for more than the mere product or service—now they want to have an interesting life, experience new aspects of life or new places, be entertained, and learn in an enjoyable way (Pine and Gilmore 2011). These are all fulfilled by experiences.

The project of experience creation may involve all or some of the following: the design, management, organization, marketing, sale, and usage of the experience (how the users receive the experience) (Newbery and Farnham 2013). How many of these are involved in the project, and to what extent, differs from experience to experience, but the project of experience creation always involves some of them: it is just their combination that varies from case to case. Two experience creation projects are rarely alike, which means that all experience projects to a certain extent are innovations, as innovations range from incremental to radical innovation. They are innovations when they come onto the market, as innovation is defined as a new combination of things that comes to market. Most of them will be incremental innovations, as only a few innovations are truly radical.

### Characteristics of Experiences

There are five differences between services and experiences:

a. Intangibility: Experiences are intangible like services; services may utilize products; experiences may utilize product(s) and service(s).

Thus, a theater experience may incorporate dining products and movie service(s).

b. Perishability: Experiences are perishable like services but continue for an extended finite duration. Experiences can be launched on demand, can be invoked, or can be triggered by an event.

c. Customizability or adoptability: Most experiences can be customized or adopted per customer inclination, preferences, or choices, which may render it more complex and costlier, respectively. Experiences can record the responses and feedback of a specific customer during a visit as an input for a possible revisit in future.

d. Composability: Most experiences are composed of subexperiences, service(s), and product(s). Cricket game may incorporate introduction to players of your choice, ongoing open food court as well as sales of sports merchandise.

e. Replicability: Experiences are replicable like services; services are rendered by processes, but experiences are rendered by projects.

## AR and VR

AR superimposes the virtual objects with real world and thus augments the physical world environment with the virtual world, leading to enhanced sensibilities of humans. One of the most familiar examples of AR is the score board displayed during live telecast of sports matches. Also, the replay of any scene of the match during live telecast is also performed using AR as it displays a view of real world with some graphical symbol (e.g., use of a line for depicting path of the ball during cricket match) produced by a computer. AR incorporates all kinds of sensorial information like auditory sensation, virtual sensation, haptic (touch-based) sensation, and olfactory (smell-based) sensation (Craig 2013).

The three fundamental characteristics of AR are:

- It combines the real with the virtual world.
- It displays real-time interactions.
- The real and virtual are displayed in 3D.

AR approach is effective and has a huge impact because it allows a person to carry out real-world's tasks using virtual information, for example, a cricket commentator can substantiate batter's play analysis by displaying in parallel (say) bowler's statistics. One of the main aspects of this technology is that it encourages interaction. Footwear brands like Nike and Gucci provide AR features to try out different shoe designs and might consider including social sharing so that consumers can instantly acquire feedback from friends (Hilken et al. 2020).

VR refers to a medium consisting of computer-generated simulations that are able to augment or replace the real world and gives the feeling of being immersed in a simulated world/virtual world to the user, that is, a user can navigate in the virtual environment in real time (just like in the physical world) (Steinicke 2016). The feedback of VR is felt via sensory perception such as haptic, auditory, and visual perception, similar to that in AR. VR incorporates various technologies, for example, AI, image processing, computer graphics, sound systems, networking, and so on (Mihelj et al. 2014).

The three fundamental characteristics of VR are:

- Imagination: User selects a scenario that does not exist, but feels being a part of that scenario because of the manipulation of sensory information by the system.
- Interaction: User selects a mode that connects him/her with the system that is often assisted by 3D feeding mediums like head-mounted device (HMD), space ball, and so on.
- Immersion: User selects a mode to experience an illusion of seamless reality incorporating multimodal sensory inputs like vision, audition, touch, and so on.

VR is an entirely computer-generated view of a world in 3D where everything in view is purely virtual, that is, everything the user sees is synthesized and not real. Immersion or *sense of being there* is a key element in VR to enable high fidelity interaction with the user to make him or her believe that the virtual world is *real* (Verma and Paul 2022). In VR, the virtual world can provide a virtual experience of either enhanced or subdued versions of *reality*. Additionally, VR provides multimodal interaction feedback to the wearer's visual, auditory, olfactory, haptic, tactile, system, and so on to get close to real experiences. Consumer

> low-cost VR HMDs are commercially available from HTC, Oculus, and Sony, among others, with high-resolution displays and tracking capabilities of the user's motions and actions.

## Types of Experiences

i. Prosaic experiences are routine, everyday, ordinary experiences whose real value is in define the baseline for minimum acceptable experiences (MAE), failing which can increase the likelihood of a poor engagement experience, for example, parking at the supermarket.

ii. Mindful experiences need the active or conscious cognitive engagement with an element of the experience. Mindful experiences are important to capture the attention of customers. To create such experiences, companies could look into injecting novelty to help break the monotony and increase mindfulness of the experience without rendering it irritable, for example, safety instructions on the airplane.

iii. Memorable experiences are important for companies because they leave a lasting impression on their customers, whether or not they support the decision-making processes for the first or subsequent purchases of the company's offerings. Memorable experiences require positive emotional engagement from customers without aggravating their anxiety on any account. For example, lost and found services at any event management location.

iv. Meaningful experiences require high emotional and cognitive involvement while ascertaining choices or preferences while engaging with element(s) of experiences. A high involvement experience that supports cocreation is common for brands that offer personalization. For instance, the *Nike by You* collection is a customizable shoe product line that allows customers to personalize the design of the shoes according to their preferences.

v. Transformational experiences usually revolve around novel experiences that customers remember and create unique associations of the company or brand in their minds. Such experiences usually lead to a shift in perspectives, behavior, or attitudes and can be evoked by a trigger, incident or inspirational speeches. These experiences are subjective, so a transformational experience for one person may only be a mindful experience for another because of the differing circumstances or personal backgrounds.

### ELC, ELM, Experience SCM, and BOProj

Experience lifecycle (ELC) is a complex network with large supply chains from multiple organizations. Lifecycle assessment of services of organizations with globally dispersed manufacturing, supply chains, and international market involves various spatial and temporal constraints.

Experience lifecycle management (ELM) is the business activity of managing, in the most effective way, a company's experiences offerings all the way across their lifecycles; from the very first idea for an experience all the way through until it is terminated or replaced.

Experience SCM involves a consistent flow of exact, timely useful information regarding basic projects, processes, products, and partnerships.

BOProj is the basis for projects execution, processes, and work schedules, and describes how projects are created from subprojects, processes, and products recursively.

## Context

A company must be able to assess and comprehend the various influences the context has on the enacted experiences for the customers so that they can be used effectively for positive outcomes (Brézillon and Gonzalez 2014).

1. Individual Level: The individual-level context comprises factors such as emotions, cognitions, physical, and economic factors. Firstly, an individual's emotions can influence his behavior, for example, a person who is happy is more receptive to trying new things, while a person who has been disappointed is more likely to see things from a negative lens. Secondly, a person's cognition can also greatly impact his perception and behavior, for example, a poor experience may result in the lack of trust and desire to re-engage with a company in the future.

2. Social Level: The social-level context refers to the social rules and norms followed by the customers and the influences from their social networks. Individuals no longer act in a social vacuum; they are in constant communication with their environment and social networks, for example, an individual's poor experience will not stay confined to himself but most likely to spread through his social network(s) by word of mouth and sharing.

3. Market Level: The market-level market context reflects the actors of the market with which the customers interact, namely, competitors, substitutes, and complementors, whose actions can influence the customer behavior. Competitors' actions such as new product launches or promotion campaigns can impact customer expectations. With the increase in the level of transparency by reason of prevalent actors like price aggregators and marketplaces, customers can compare prices and information more easily and switch readily with the reduced costs. In the early days, customers were more brand loyal as a result of the information asymmetry, which was perceived as a dampener to the higher risk of switching.

4. Environment Level: The environment-level context refers to the macroenvironment constituted of political, economic, environmental, and technological factors within which the customers operate. The environmental context has a significant impact on customer behavior as every individual customer functions within a broader environment, for example, while the global COVID-19 pandemic resulted in lower consumption levels due to the unstable economic conditions, it also led to a higher-level of consumption on daily necessities due to the work-from-home and stay-at-home phenomenon.

## TRIZ, or the Theory of Inventive Problem-Solving

TRIZ (pronounced *treez*) is the Russian abbreviation of what can be translated as *the theory of inventive problem-solving*. TRIZ is used by companies as the primary methodology for innovation of offerings, that is, products, services, and experiences.

TRIZ was developed by Genrich Saulovich Altshuller (1926–1998) who was interested in basing creativity on science. TRIZ was unknown outside the USSR until the 1990s, and its popularity in the United States, Japan, and the Pacific Rim, and Western Europe has been growing rapidly. Many Fortune 500 companies have cited a phenomenal increase in productivity, and they credit TRIZ for the breakthrough ideas and quality solutions to tough engineering problems as fueling that increase. TRIZ is based on the analysis of a vast number of inventions (40,000) and on the attempt to induce general rules and principles that explain how a designer can creatively tackle a problem in order to generate inventive solutions (Altshuller 1984).

Additional details are available in the Appendix section (**A.7.3 TRIZ, or the Theory of Inventive Problem-Solving**) available online.

## Conclusion

This chapter presented an overview of the three avatars of a startup's offering, namely, product, service, and experience. The chapter began with description of the various stages of the PLC as also the attributes and approaches for the design of products. The chapter then described the characteristics and types of services. Experience invariably is constituted of interactions between the provider and the customer or consumer; interaction is influenced by three influence factors, namely, human, system, and context. The latter part of the chapter describes the characteristics and types of experiences. It highlighted how a company must be able to assess and comprehend the various influences the context has on the enacted experiences for the customers or consumers so that they can be used effectively for resulting in positive outcomes. The chapter ended with a description of TRIZ, which is the theory of inventive problem-solving for generating and continuously innovating the products, services, or experiences offered by a startup.

*This chapter presented an overview of the products, services, and experiences forming the core offerings provided by the startup. While introducing AR and VR solutions, it highlighted that products can be mass produced for customers. Services can be mass customized for customer preferences and experiences can be mass innovated for customer preferences.*

# CHAPTER 8

# Structure

## Topics Covered

- Organizational Structure
  - Organization
    - *Network Organization Model*
- Virtual Organization
  - Network Businesses
  - Virtual Organization and Outsourcing
  - Collaboration Networks
  - Alliance Networks
- Network of Projects
  - Decision Making for Selection of Projects
  - Project Management

## Introduction

*This chapter presents aspects of organizational structures that are most conducive for periods of diverse, high-intensity resources and efforts, and when required, also of explosive growth. It gives an overview of the efficacy of network structures as embodied in real-life network of projects, including with partners and alliances.*

## Organization Structure

As enterprises search for ways of increasing the speed, flexibility, integration, and innovation of their firms, they first focus on its structure. Firms want to know what are the eligible structural options and what will work best for their firms (Mintzberg 1979). Firm structures observed in mature organizations are mainly rooted in the classical organization theory characterized by principles of scientific management. Based on these principles, organizations were structured primarily to reflect economies of scale and standardization of work. This so-called mechanistic perspective gave rise to the functional organization structure. Further thinking about organizations emerged based on the view that organizations were primarily systems, that is, a change in one part of the system will produce different effects in the system as a whole. And because the operating environment of firms changes frequently, interactions within a system are inherently complex. Typical structures reflecting early systems thinking are divisional (product, process, geographic/market, or customer) and matrix. Later, systems thinking and complexity theories related to firms have resulted in structures that aim to enable self-organizing and interacting networks of agents. Structures reflecting open systems and complexity theories include network (of projects) and cluster.

The various kinds of firm structures are (Waterman, Peters, and Phillips 1980):

1. Functional structure is a highly traditional structure deriving from the Taylorist view of organizations and is often found in strong command and control organizations such as the military. The key strategy of functionally focused organizations is to maximize margins through leveraging economies of scale and functional expertise.

2. Divisional structure

   Product structure is the most appropriate in a business where there are low synergies between the buyers and the distribution channels of the different divisions. Typically, in this structure, each division runs as an independent business unit.

   Processes structure is most appropriate in a business where the core services are shared and operated across the firm. Internal support services are frequently organized in this way, but customer-facing services are equally well served by this structure, which is a good alternative to the functional structure.

   Customer structure is the most appropriate in a business where the customer segments are clearly defined by need, economics, distribution, and other key attributes.

3. Matrix structure is most appropriate in a business where they typically operate in two dimensions (e.g., function and product). The aim of the matrix structure is to provide customers with innovative solutions through effective teams of highly skilled individuals.

4. Team structure is most appropriate in a business where they are *on loan* from their respective functional departments and are thus assigned full time for the team's leader in tackling high-priority and short-term durations assignments or tasks.

5. Network structure is the most appropriate in a business where they are fast-moving organizations that are highly innovative and operating in an environment that requires speed, flexibility, and high levels of customer focus. In network firms, work is typically organized around team and projects delivery, because different projects have distinctively different ways of working; however, as the projects work in coherence, the delivery to the customer is seamless.

6. Virtual structures is the most appropriate in a business where independent firms join together their efforts for a committed period to render a service to an outgoing activity or execute a project and then dissolve. This type of organizational structure is only possible because of communication technology.

### Organization

Organizing means arranging and relating work so that it can be done efficiently by the appropriate people. Efficiency is achieved by a proper partition and distribution of work, as well as suitable coordination between the various groups of people participating in the work that is subject to the constraints of time, resources, and business priority. Organization is either used as a noun or as a verb. As a noun, it refers to a type of institution or social structure. And, as a verb, it refers to a type of system of action (Kates and Galbriath, 2007; Daft 2020). The institutional perspective sees organizations as entities that exist independently of the constituting people and have a life over and above the life of their individual members (Keathley and Harrington 2020). By contrast, the action perspective sees organizations as entities that are constructed continually or recreated through the continuing actions of their constituting members.

This implies that in the action view, organizations do not exist independently of its constituting people and do not have a life independent of the actions of their individual members. Both of these opposing point of views on organization can be reconciled if we treat organization not as a state of being but of becoming. Organization is best seen a complex system in which structure emerges from action.

An organization as a structure can be seen to emerge from the continuing pattern of actions performed by its constituting members. Thus, organization's institutional and action perspectives are not incompatible—organizations are both institutions and collective of actions. Through member interaction, organizational structures are created but may also be changed. Members utilize organizational structure in interpreting their own and other people's actions—organization structure acts as a constraint on member action. Through such a process of configuration, an organization is constituted and reconstituted. A role is defined as a bundle of actions that are appropriate in particular circumstances; much like organizational routines, roles guide decisions about what actions to take. Similarly, organizational domain is a coherent collection of patterns of actions. Defining organizations in terms of patterns of actions taken by both people and technical actors enables reframing organizations as sociotechnical organizations.

Complex systems are made of autonomous agents that are typically decentralized and independent entities. Inspired by nature, for a better control of the whole system, the number of information and links that can be processed effectively is limited to control the resultant complexity. Any system or network is characterized by:

- A tree structure
- Multiplication of organizational levels
- Speciation of components

As most components or agents possess their own autonomy and are also strongly interconnected, the consequences of centralized and hierarchical controller architectures using dynamic and fully distributed (or heterarchical) scheduling with intelligent components can be analyzed.

Accordingly, steering structures can be divided into type of organizations (Table 8.1).

   a. Centralized organizations are those with traditional centralized command and control architectures. A centralized control unit collates, manages, and controls all production and delivery units.

   b. Decentralized organizations are classified into three type of architectures:

- Hierarchical architectures (e.g., projects constituted of multiple skill-teams)
- Heterarchical architectures include both centralized or distributed structures (e.g., projects constituted of centralized or distributed skill teams)
- Hybrid architectures include both hierarchical (e.g., projects constituted of multiple skill teams) and heterarchical structures (e.g., projects constituted of centralized or distributed skill-teams) simultaneously

*Table 8.1  Decentralized versus centralized system characteristics*

| Characteristic | Centralized | Decentralized |
|---|---|---|
| Control | Central | Distributed |
| Scalability | Low | High |
| Failures | Single point | No single point |
| Stability | Low | High |
| Vulnerable | Yes | No |
| Design | Easy | Difficult |
| Maintenance | Easy | Difficult |

Network Organization Model

A network organization is a coalition of firms that work collectively and collaboratively to create value for the customers of a focal firm (Daft 2007; Recardo 2008). Sometimes, the coalition is loosely connected; at other times, it is tightly defined, as in the relationship between Dell and its component suppliers. An network organization consists of a wide range of companies—suppliers, joint venture (JV) partners, contractors, distributors, franchisees, licensees, and so on—that contribute to the focal firm's creation and delivery of value to its customers. Each of these firms in turn will have their own network organizations focused around themselves. Thus, relationships between firms in the network both enable and constrain focal companies in the achievement of their goals (Veldsman 2019).

American and European companies that had been creating cartels after the Second World War are considered pioneers of network organizations. Formation of network structures are formed because of the network connections or mutually beneficial interorganizational dependencies.

Such cooperation materializes because of many factors:

i. Globalization of markets
ii. Changes in the environment and context in terms of changes in relevant technologies
iii. Competition in their sector(s) of business
iv. Adoption of various best practices that are native to different firms constituting the network

Network connections or mutually beneficial interorganizational dependencies arise for a number of reasons:

- To provide information
- To reduce uncertainty
- To provide flexibility
- To enable speed of responses to seize opportunities quickly and comprehensively
- To provide access to resources and skills especially if it possesses requisite complementary assets
- To provide ready capacity

There are four types of network organizations, namely, transactional networks, value-added networks, flexible networks, and virtual networks. The transactional network is a transaction-based firm competing in a highly competitive environment and uses the transactional relationships to link customers with goods and services that meets their needs via an extensive network of suppliers and buyers (i.e., customers). Firm forming a value-added network compete on markets where preferences are diffused and market segments are difficult to define. This type utilizes a global network of suppliers combined with a substantial internal operations. A flexible network organization is usually found under the conditions of high environmental volatility, but has intranetwork links that are cooperative and long-lasting (Moretti 2017). This type is characterized by communication links between the focal and the node firms, but each node firm operates independently by performing the tasks agreed with the focal company. A virtual organization (VO) is a reformed version of a traditional firm.

As firms have experienced the need to be simultaneously efficient, flexible, responsive, and adaptive, they have turned increasingly to the network organization model with the following characteristics:

a. Instead of holding all assets required to produce a given product or service in-house, networks, use the collective assets of several firms located along the value chain.

b. Networks rely more on market mechanisms rather than on administrative processes to manage resource flows. These mechanisms are not simple arms-length relationships usually associated with independently owned economic entities. Instead, to maintain the position within the network, members recognize their interdependence and are willing to share information, cooperate with each other, and customize their product or service.

c. While a network of subcontractors has been common for many years, recently formed networks expect members to play a much more proactive role in improving the final product or service.

## VOs

VOs are alliances between firms that join forces for a limited time to realize specific brands or fulfil specific orders or even accomplish specific tasks. The goals are determined solely by the objectives of their current focal firm. Certain technical prerequisites need to be met so as to ensure these VOs can function without being tethered to a particular location. The immense economic and strategic advantage of this form of organization lies in its flexibility to respond rapidly and at short notices to the changes in the marketplace (Rijmenam van 2020; Sztipanovits and Ying 2020).

A VO differs from the strategic alliance, in that it places emphasis not on how two or more firms can work together to their mutual benefit but on how a focal firm can be created with flexible boundaries and ownership aided by the facilities provided by electronic data exchange and communication. Instead of organizational learning, the basic objective of a VO is the creation of a flexible organization of firms, with each carrying out one or more functions in order to deliver a competitive product to the customer. This necessitates a clear understanding among all participating units of the VO, the current central objectives of the VO. In the absence of such an understanding, there is a high risk that the VO will lack the will and purpose to compete successfully with more integrated corporations.

The risk of vulnerability when working within a VO is illustrated by a well-known example where an innovation partnership operating in a virtual fashion actually works against the long-term interests of the focal firm. When IBM, although far from being a VO itself, decided to develop and make its PC in a virtual manner, it coupled its hardware with Microsoft's software and an Intel microprocessor. This gave Microsoft and Intel the impetus to grow from small beginnings to become larger than IBM itself. Consequently, IBM missed the opportunity to make the microprocessor and develop the software in-house, which it certainly had the resources to do. Instead, it effectively gave away some of its core competencies.

Additional details are available in the Appendix section (**A.8.1 VOs**) available online.

## Network of Projects

As the rate of change increases, enterprises have to look for greater agility, flexibility, and innovation from their companies. Instead of pursuing strategies, structures, and cultures that are designed to create a traditional three to five years' strategy window, companies must seek a string of temporary competitive advantages through an approach to organization design that assumes change is normal, that is, Built_for_Change or transformable enterprises. Thus, the need for on-demand changes in organization structure and operations, and, excellence, is much more a function of possessing the ability for both flexible as well as fundamental changes. Enterprises need to be built around structures and practices that routinely encourage change and not thwart it, that is, projects.

Once the strategy of an enterprise is finalized, the main task of leadership is managing the realization and execution of this strategy, that is, business management by transforming all organizations primarily into a network of projects.

### Decision Making for Selection of Projects

Traditional techniques for preselection ranking of projects are described as follows:

a. Categorical Methods: These types of methods are basically qualitative methods based on historical data. After the evaluation of the projects based on the criteria, the sponsor gives an overall rating. This method is a clear and systematic way of ranking the projects.

b. Cost–Ratio Method: In this method, project selection is done on the basis of the cost of procuring the resources for each of the projects. The cost ratio is calculated as percentage on the basis of total individual cost and total value of procurement. The cost ratios are ascertained for different ranking criteria such as delivery, cost, quality, and so on. A list of such criteria is given as follows:
   - Delivery
   - Cost
   - Quality
   - Performance history
   - Technical capability
   - Quality performance
   - Geographical location
   - Financial position
   - Procedural compliance

c. Linear Averaging or Weighted Point Method: In this method, the sponsor decides on the factors that are to be selected as important for project selection. The sponsor assigns the weightage for each factor and then the project performance is decided for each of the factors selected.

As project selection involves a number of alternative projects and is based on a number of criteria, this can be addressed by multicriteria decision analysis (MCDA) techniques:

- Simple multiattribute rating technique (SMART)
- Analytic hierarchy process (AHP)
- Analytic network process (ANP)
- Data envelopment analysis (DEA)
- Elimination Et Choix Traduisant la Realité (ELECTRE): Elimination and choice translating reality
- Multiattribute utility theory (MAUT)
- Multiattribute value theory (MAVT)
- Preference ranking organization method for enrichment of evaluations (PROMETHEE)
- ViseKriterijumskaOptimizcijaiKaompromisnoResenje (VIKOR)

## Project Management

The attention of the organization shifts from that of business and organizational planning to execution (Ken Burnett 1998; Richardson 2019; Pinto 2016). Most organizations experience difficulties in managing projects, but following a good project management methodology can help alleviate many of these issues without encumbering the project manager's flexibility (Project Management Institute 2021; Ellis 2016). A sound project management methodology helps to solve the human problems that occur in any project and results in project team members:

i. Understanding their roles in the project
ii. Being motivated and willing to accept personal commitments
iii. Knowing how to delegate effectively and how to share responsibility when appropriate

Complementary to the use of a methodology is the appointment of a skilled and competent project manager who is essential to the success of any project. Traditionally, project management has been assisted by a set of technical tools that are excellent planning, scheduling, and control tools to assist a manager (such as PERT, which is essentially event-driven, or CPM which is essentially activity- (or task-) driven) (Kerzner 2017).

Traditionally, systems development methodologies identify what has to be done and the evidence of the required skilled tasks and the corresponding resources. By contrast, project management methodology emphasizes the importance of people (i.e., who is concerned and who should be concerned about what does and does not get done) by emphasizing a clear understanding of the roles and responsibilities of all project stakeholders. Consequently, project management uses the personal commitment, drive, and energy of project members to ensure the successful completion of the projects. These personal commitments are both the driving force and the controlling component of all project work. Thus, an essential element in successful project management is maintenance of each responsible individual's feeling of commitment toward the success of the project at every instance.

The fact that every enterprise needs a PM is flagged by the following facts:

- Rising overhead and increasing complexity
- Slow cycle time on getting new products from idea to launch
- Uneven (start-and-stop) project activity
- Overwhelmed and overtasked project managers
- Lengthy and unproductive project review meetings
- A perpetual scarcity of project resources, with senior management time wasted in disputes between project managers and resource managers
- Frustration among project participants over the lack of project results
- Executive concerns about the organization's ability to deliver on critical new projects

## Project Lifecycle

The project management lifecycle is constituted of four phases:

1. Project Initiation: The primary purpose of the initiation phase is to determine the optimal approach to execute the project after conducting a thorough evaluation on the implementation feasibility of the project and to ensure the continual support of the organization. During this phase, project members utilize a wide range of assessment and evaluation tools, such as stakeholder identification and assessment, risk identification and evaluation, initial requirement analysis, and estimation of scope, resources, and cost. The cumulation of this work is a project charter—a contract between the sponsor, representing the customers and executives, and the project manager, representing the project team. For selective projects, there can be further analysis on organizational readiness and adoption, evaluation of conflicts including politics, and impact on operations.

   The initiation of a project is triggered by identification of a new potential project through a proposal for the same. The project definition or scope is obtained by an overview of the project through a list of committed deliverables (with a corresponding list of necessary fitness-for-purpose features), collateral targeted outcomes, and consequent downstream subprojects or processes. It is here that a number of core parameters are established and confirmed with the funding authority. The project analysis commences with a tentative script for project execution including stakeholders, risks, issues, and governance aspects. This preliminary script is then used to derive tentative estimates of duration and cost. By setting scope in this way, the work and resources for the project are completely bounded. With scope locked down, any uncertainty about time and cost in the eventual project charter can arise only from uncertainty in estimates of parameters.

A carefully considered statement of scope provides a robust foundation for recognizing, analyzing, and resolving issues of *scope creep* (the tendency for projects to grow in size over time).

The results of the analysis together with the project definition and relevant contextual details are incorporated into a project charter that is submitted for endorsement to the funding authority. The project charter establishes bounds on these parameters, outside of which the project sponsor will require the approval of the funding authority. Initiation ends with a decision by the funding authority to either accept or reject the project charter as a baseline foundational reference for project planning.

2. Project Planning: The purpose of the planning phase is to drive as much clarity as possible and prepare project teams before organizations commit to significant resources required in the subsequent phase of project execution. This is achieved through the appropriate level of planning for the project. The analysis that underpins planning is a significantly more detailed and thorough version of that completed during initiation—with the objective of producing much more reliable estimates of timeframes and costs. The project plan, together with the project definition appearing in the business case, provides a baseline to project execution (Callahan, Stetz, and Brooks 2011).

In the traditional predictive project management approach, the requirement for specificity is much higher than for the iterative or Agile approach. In adaptive project management approach, the overall project plan is prepared by analyzing factors such as the feasibility of modular implementation, the number of iterations, the duration of each iteration, customer review, and the dedicated core team responsible to drive the completion of the project. As details of future iterations emerge, increasingly detailed planning and preparation occurs repeatedly at the beginning of each iteration. Hybrid project management approaches adopt a stance that balances the need for clarity with demonstrating early results and getting early customer feedback.

The prime focus of planning is on development of a script of project execution. To ensure high reliability of the planning process, planning takes the committed deliverables and all endogenous downstream processes and analyses iteratively:

a. Assemble a work breakdown structure (WBS), which is a model of the work required to produce each of the project's committed deliverables, along with a supporting Gantt chart. WBS can be employed to estimate the duration of the work involved in the production of all project's deliverables. This is obtained by estimating the duration of each task and noting any dependencies among those tasks. Consequently, the duration of execution is also estimated.

b. Estimate internal and external resources guided by the Gantt chart and typically past experiences of analogous projects, and develop an initial resources schedule in the form of tables showing what resources are required and when (resource breakdown structure (RBS)). Consequently, the overall cost of execution is estimated, and a cash flow projection is developed for the project (cost breakdown structure (CBS)).

c. Relevant details from both the Gantt chart and the resource schedules can then be combined into a milestones schedule. Consequently, this schedule will become the basic reference for judging the progress of the project during the subsequent project execution phase reviews.

Where,

- WBS is in the form of a hierarchical list of all the work packages involved in a particular work.
- Gantt chart is a calendar-based diagram incorporating three parts, namely, start date, duration, and finish date.
- Critical path is a chain of linked tasks that, if not completed on time, will necessarily delay the finish date of a project by the same duration of time. Tasks on the critical path are identified as *critical tasks* and should be monitored closely by the project manager during execution because any delay with these will cause the whole project to finish later than planned.
- Slack or float is the amount by which the duration of a task can be extended, without causing the project to be delayed. The critical path can also be viewed as the sequence of tasks with zero slack. Project managers can use tasks with large slack to increase their flexibility in planning. For example,

resources from such activities may be moved to activities on the critical path, if this can result in shorter overall project duration.

---

The bulk of a project's costs is incurred during execution as resources are deployed (or purchased). Because it is cumulative, the planned expenditure graph rises monotonically and, hence, is often referred to as an $S$ curve ($S$ in this case stands for *sigmoid*—indicating that it often takes on a shape suggestive of a stretched letter $S$). The relationship between project duration and cost appears somewhat counterintuitive. Neither cost nor duration can be manipulated directly, but both are sensitive to changes in the application of high-cost (premium) resources applied to tasks in the WBS—which can be manipulated by the project manager. In general, if premium resources are withdrawn selectively from a task, its cost will decrease, but its duration will increase so that it appears that the duration is falling in response to a cost increase. If, on the other hand, additional premium resources are selectively applied to a task, its cost will increase, but its duration will decrease so that it appears that the duration is increasing in response to a cost decrease.

---

For every task in the WBS, an earliest feasible finish date can be derived. While milestones are finish events that are supported with evidence of achievability, deadlines are set arbitrarily without any supporting evidence of achievability. As execution can be tracked meaningfully only by using milestones, project managers are required to replace all deadlines with milestones before finalizing a project plan. In the situation when a project has an arbitrarily short deadline that is in conflict with that implied by the WBS and Gantt chart, majorly three options are available to address this, namely, increasing the rate at which extra resources are made available for selected tasks, descoping the project, and relaxing the deadline. Similarly, in the situation when the established budget is arbitrarily smaller than that implied by analysis of the resources demanded by the project, majorly four options are available to address this, namely, substituting nonpremium rate resources for premium cost resources, descoping the project, enhancing the budget, and scaling back any risk management plan that had been adopted.

In the finalized project plan used as the baseline for the project execution phase, while the benefits sought by the funding authority from the project planning would normally remain as declared in the project charter, estimates of other variables used in the investment decision may change, namely, costs, disbenefits, and risks. This is true not only for the values of these estimates but also their reliability.

3. Project Execution: The project execution phase is generally the most expensive and most resource intensive as also the longest duration of all the phases. As a part of project execution, project managers spend a considerable amount of time monitoring the progress of their projects, comparing the actual with the planned, and making adjustments to control the process and the outcome. Consequently, controlling becomes the primary function of management because most complex endeavors require proactive steering and adjustment during the course of the project execution.

The execution phase tends to dominate a project in terms of work, elapsed time, and expenditure and is constituted of three sequential subprocesses, namely, project setup, production of deliverables, and execution wind-up. The first of these relates to producing and implementing the list of project setup deliverables that appear in the statement of project scope. Because these serve as infrastructure in support of overall execution, they will be scheduled for production at predetermined times. Finally, when all of the deliverables that are in the project scope have been delivered, the project execution infrastructure and administration setup is disbanded.

4. Project Closure: The project transition and/or closure phase winds down the project and transitions the deliverables to another project or to operations. The closure and transition activities include finishing the list of tasks, obtaining sponsor or customer signoff, demobilizing the project team and reallocating resources, paying project vendors, conducting lessons learned, updating key project deliverables and artifacts, transferring project knowledge to operational teams, and preparing for the final project report.

# Conclusion

Given the modern business environment, businesses need to more proactively create structures that can deliver greater agility. Enterprises in search for ways of increasing the speed, flexibility, integration, and innovation of their firms must necessarily focus on its structure. Strict hierarchies get very good at exploiting existing advantage but are pretty terrible at being responsive to rapid change and embedding exploration and experimentation into the fabric of how they work. The big opportunity is that, aside from the ability to deliver business as usual and optimize existing advantage via traditional hierarchies, we can use small, multidisciplinary teams to accentuate a more networked element to the business.

*This chapter presented aspects of organizational structures that are most conducive for periods of diverse, high-intensity resources and efforts, and when required, also of explosive growth. It gave an overview of the efficacy of network structures as embodied in real-life network of projects, including with partners and alliances.*

# CHAPTER 9

# Staff

## Topics Covered

- Human Resources Management in Startups
- Team Based Management
  - Stages of Team Building
    - Initiating Stage
    - Formative Stage
    - Functional Stage
    - Productive Stage
  - Team Organization Elements
  - Team Decision Making
- Not Human Resources but Talent Management
  - Talent Management
- Employee Engagement
- Teams and Innovation

## Introduction

*This chapter presents the aspects of building high-performance teams, including team-based management, not human resources but talent management, role-based rather than function-based responsibilities, employee engagement, team building, personnel and team performance management, and so on. This chapter highlights a factor that is very critical for a startup: long-run consistent productive results are always delivered by the optimal effort of a team and not by a team of superhuman individuals. Also, a team working together can overcome all possible encountered problems easily—there is no need for every member to have every useful ability or skill.*

## Human Resources Management in Startups

Human resources management (HRM) commonly consists of the following activities (Machado and Davim 2019):

- People resourcing
- HR planning
- Learning, training, and development
- Performance management
- Reward management
- Diversity and inclusion
- Engagement and branding
- Employee relations
- Administration and compliance

At the beginning, startup firms are characterized by technically and/or entrepreneurially oriented founders that work in close relation with their employees who are also completely dedicated to the product (development) and the firm. Communication is immediate and informal. The more successful the company is at that stage, the more likely growth becomes an issue. In particular, in fast-growing firms, entrepreneurs are challenged by introducing formal processes and get burdened with managerial tasks. The success factors of early stages become pitfalls in subsequent ones. Whereas a hardworking founder deeply involved in operative activities is important to survive the first years and bring his or her vision to reality, the ability of taking over a more managerial role or pass this responsibility on to somebody specialist in the field becomes essential.

Adaption of the organizational structure is especially critical for young firms as they are most susceptible to the adverse effects of an inappropriate organizational structure as their resource base is limited and their organizational slack resources are small. Basically, the culture of open informal communication enables a good climate of working together; however, difficulties in sharing information and knowledge appear with growth. Growing startups are confronted with a very special situation: They are no longer small enough to manage their duties informally, and they are not large enough to have such formalized ways like a global corporation.

Growing startups take over an intermediate position. It is critical to the success that they formalize their processes; otherwise, they are threatened to decline as the flexibility and spontaneity that formerly brought the success now resulted in confusion, insecurity, and inefficiency. However, it is crucial to the success to be aware of not losing the incentives that are important for knowledge workers—flexibility, spontaneity, autonomy, and a collaborative working environment.

Knowledge worker in high-technology companies has the following characteristics:

- High qualification, as high-technology companies focus on the research and exploration of some technology in a specific area and, in consequence, need edge knowledge of this area.
- Strong motivation, as knowledge staff has clear objectives, and they expect to exert their specialties and wisdom to gain achievements in work, not only to fulfill a stable objective.
- Sense of independence, derived from having a high qualification in a specific area.
- Creative spirit, as it is necessary for this work.
- Communication and participation skills, as knowledge staff intend to be open minded to others' opinions and they prefer to communicating and participating more than others.
- Frequent job movements, as they are more tied to their profession than to their company.
- Difficulty in evaluation, as work is often collective and, in consequence, it is not easy to assess the individual contribution.

Consequently, it gets more and more decisive to tie knowledge workers to the firm to reach ambitious business objectives and shape the firm's future. In particular, in periods of economic highs, small enterprises with limited resources have to find ways to retain their best employees. Also, the current shift in demographics and the consequent potential lack of workforce raise the challenge of how to recruit and retain good employees. Difficulty in recruiting qualified staff is a main barrier for SME's innovative capacity what makes it even more important to position oneself as attractive employer although compensation cannot be the motivator comparing to larger competitors.

Sustaining the role-based design characterized by flexibility, collaboration, innovation, and informal communication is central to attracting and maintaining the knowledge workers that are able to come up with innovative high-tech products (Machado and Davim 2014).

i. Knowledge workers: Such a role design fits well with the requirements of knowledge workers, and thus, they are highly autonomously motivated.

ii. Informal communication: As technology startups are confronted with high environmental dynamics, this is one of the most important strengths. Based on a low degree of formal rules for communication, information can flow extremely fast in a very informal way.

iii. Collaborative working environment: Project-based role-based working, as it is common in technology startups, fosters a collaborative working environment. As different competences are required for developing high-tech products, collaboration and cooperation are essential. This is enabled by a common vision based on the founder's principles.

iv. Flexibility: Based on a comparatively low degree of bureaucracy, HRM in technology startups is able to flexibly react to changing environment—which is an enormous competitive advantage compared to larger organizations with a more inflexible HRM system. They are flexible due to people working on service contracts but also by reason of their case-by-case decisions about training activities outside the firm. Moreover, allocating HR internally between projects enables fast reactions.

v. Innovative climate: Knowledge workers carry the dedication to find out something new. Combined with the vision of the founder that directs their search and the possibility to exchange ideas informally in- or outside the projects leads to an innovative climate. Moreover, a culture that sees failures as inherent in the innovation process facilitates new product development enormously.

Most difficulties arise when the firm grows in employees, sales, products, or market segments, and thus, the requirements to the HRM system and the organization as a whole change. The previous strengths, which fostered organizational success and growth, can easily switch to weaknesses and endanger the survival of the firm:

i. Top Management as HR Agent: In technology startups, the top managers are usually not trained in HRM because they primarily enjoyed a technical education. As they focus on technology, they spend only little time and effort on HRM and on developing their skills in this field. Therefore, they often do not realize the importance of these issues and lose sight of necessary changes.

ii. Control Mechanisms: Knowledge workers enjoy working autonomously, and performance is secured by clan control. However, as proper project documentation or tracking of working hours is missing, there is a certain insecurity on side of the top management—especially when the firm grows and keeping an overview over activities gets more difficult.

iii. Structures and Rules: It is possible that the preferred autonomy and independence switch to a great burden for employees that later enter the firm as there are no rules and structures they can follow. The larger the firm gets, the more interpretations of how the daily processes should be pursued exist. This is reflected by different performance norms or understanding of communication and collaboration, which causes conflicts and insecurity.

Factors that foster a successful HR system in small technology firms are as follows:

a. Top management needs to:
   - Be aware of the employees' needs
   - Foster and support employees
   - Provide a high level of trust to employees
   - Be open for continuous development and change
b. Corporate culture needs to support:
   - Collaboration
   - Creativity
   - Autonomy

- Failures
- Flexibility

c. Employees need to be:
  - Independent and autonomous
  - Innovative and creative
  - Proactive and self-dependent
  - Enthusiastic about the product
  - Highly committed to the firm
  - Open for continuous development and change

## Team-Based Management

People play a significant role in the success of a firm. Staffing function has gained increasing importance because acquiring and retaining talent has emerged as a key competitive advantage for a firm. Staffing is an activity that involves all actions that ensure filling and sustaining all positions in an organizational structure (Kaschny and Nolden 2018).

The primary focus of staffing is on acquiring and retaining right people at the right positions in the organization at the right time. On the basis of the plan and objectives of the enterprise, the number and types of the employees that would be required in an organization are required. The requirement for the HR are compared with the available talent through the management inventory to determine the gaps and surpluses. Based on this analysis, internal and external resources are utilized for recruiting, selecting, training, allocating, appraising, promoting, or separation of excess manpower.

There is a fundamental difference between groups and its refined version in the form of teams. In a group, members work independently toward their individual goals because group goals and beliefs are not binding on its members. Consequently, while performing their roles, members focus only on enhancing individual excellence. Members are mistrustful of each other and prefer to hold back their contribution to the group goals; they are apprehensive of any difference of opinions or perspectives because any disagreement is interpreted as a threat to their position in the group.

By contrast, in a team, members work interdependently toward the common team goals through which they also realize their individual goals. Consequently, while performing their roles, they feel a sense of ownership toward their role because they are committed to the accomplishment of the team's goals. Members collaborate and use their experience and skills to contribute to the success of the team goals; members are even willing to sacrifice their personal goals if required for the accomplishment of the team goals. The cornerstone of the team's success is mutual trust among the members who make a conscious effort to respect and understand individual perspectives; members feel good about contributing to the achievement of team's goals. Members interpret differences as different ways to resolve the problems.

Advantages of team-based management are:

1. Establishes a collective responsibility and accountability of the team in accomplishing the team goal
2. Enables high involvement of all members while pursuing team goals
3. Enables increased acceptance of members with varying backgrounds and better understanding of differing perspectives and assessments on issues critical for the success of the team efforts
4. Enables contributions from members in terms of a large number and better ideas for more effective and efficient efforts in accomplishing the team goals
5. Enables infusing a sense of security in members by mutually compensating for the weaknesses of individual members
6. Facilitates successful execution of even complex tasks that cannot be addressed by individual members without a collective, coordinated, and cooperated multiskilled effort
7. Enhances the ability of successful adaptation or adoption of the ever-changing market environment, which cannot be addressed by individual members without a collective and collaborative multiskilled effort

Disadvantages of team-based management are:

1. Expends more effort and time via a team effort compared to individual-level efforts

2. Increased demand of communication between members may result in increased conflicts by reason of differing perceptions or opinions

3. Higher possibility of nominating substandard talent without attracting direct blame for the subsequent below-par performance

4. Increased likelihood of weak performances going unnoticed or unaccounted because team-based outcomes cannot be attributed directly to the responsible defaulters

5. Increased possibility of a few members bearing the full burden of the team effort for nonperformance or indifferent involvement on the part of subperforming members

### Team Development

Teams are formed for synergy, that is, to accomplish more than individuals can accomplish separately. However, the benefits of synergistic teamwork cannot be reaped right after employees have been allocated to teams because it takes time for individuals to feel comfortable in a team-based environment.

Teams need time to improve their interpersonal and technical skills related to the team activities, which are dependent upon:

- Team types like problem-solving versus developmental, project versus permanent, autonomous versus semiautonomous, and so on
- Team interpersonal development to enhance skills in communication, decision making, and conflict resolution
- Team learning curve

The focus of teams is to improve quantity and/or quality of outputs. The basic tenet of work teams is that jobs and organizations should be designed around processes instead of functions, and that the basic production unit should be the team and not the individual. Fully mature work teams set their own work goals and perform all the tasks associated with the work process.

It is important to realize that an organization should make significant investments in both technical and interpersonal training to help team members maximize their potential as a team and avoid some of the conflicts and pitfalls that hinder team development.

### Stages of Team Building

People allocated to a team do not automatically become a team the moment the assignment commences; the leader plays an important role in facilitating the transformation of the team. Top management support is critical to team implementation, especially during the formative and functional stages of development. As it takes time for the synergistic effects of teams to emerge, senior management must be patient and willing to expend the resources it takes to develop the team. Results may not be immediately forthcoming. Also, middle managers sometimes thwart team implementations efforts because they feel that their role in the organization will no longer be needed, or they are uncomfortable adjusting their role to the new team environment (Kuratko et al. 2019).

The team goes through five stages of development as a team:

1. Initiating Stage: This is the stage when a team is brought together for the first time. In the beginning, it is simply a group of people with their differing perspectives, motivations, and talents. When each member understands their contribution and responsibility to the assignment, only then a team can be formed, and work can be coordinated among the members. The cocreation of objectives ensures the participation of team members in developing the objectives of the team; it creates involvement empowerment and a sense of ownership of objectives in the team members.

2. Formative Stage: This is the stage where the detailed planning of the assignment and working of a team begins. The team leader enables clarity on the importance of the team goals and the role of member's contribution to the success of the assignment.

3. Functional Stage: This is the stage when a properly managed group begins to emerge as a team. During this stage, the gap between the reality and the expectations of the members discovered during the formative stage is progressively nullified, and the team leader encourages the group to take risks and to work through their disagreements rather

than avoiding them. The team leader needs to reinforce the assignment goals and individual member's contribution in achieving it.

4. Productive Stage: This is the stage when a properly managed group becomes a high-performing and productive team: the team provides its own direction and encouragement, deals constructively with conflicts, and acts responsibly to complete its assignments. A responsible team is a trusting team that openly admits mistakes and undertakes corrective actions.

5. Creative Stage: This is the stage where the optimum level of participation of the members and effective achievement of the goals of the assignment are accomplished. The team members continuously work and stretch themselves to create convergence about what needs to be achieved and how that has to be accomplished. At this stage, it is the individual member's sense of accomplishment that motivates them.

### Team Decision Making

Decisions by teams have many advantages over those made by individuals. An individual may be constrained by the limits of ability to gather information, ability to integrate information and professional expertise to interpret the information. In a team environment, individuals bring together a broader base of skills, effort, experience, and expertise. In an organization, all decisions are interrelated and must be coordinated with a view to achieving the overall goals of the company. These local outcomes are generally calculated not directly by benefit but by consistency, cost-effectiveness, performance, productivity, and so on. It is an essential goal for individual operational units and their managers to produce good results for local outcomes.

A decision is the result of a process intended to assess the relative benefits or merits of a set of alternatives available to determine the most advisable course of action for implementation. The decision-making process usually consists of a sequence of six activities:

i. Identify the problem and outline the goals to be achieved. These goals serve as criteria against which to compare different alternatives for solving the problem.

ii. Gather the data that is necessary to solve the problem.

iii. Generate alternatives to achieve the goals based on the data collected. An alternative is a candidate solution for the problem.

iv. Elaborate the problem by using the appropriate model, integrating all the data and decision criteria together to evaluate the alternatives.

v. Evaluate the alternatives using the model. Based on the decision criteria, the best alternative is selected.

vi. Execute the decision actions after considering practical implications and limitations.

Periodically, the team should evaluate the efficacy of the team decision process itself in light of the accumulating data on successful or failed decisions.

Certain important elements that are common to all problems are:

- Courses of Action: There are a number of possible courses of action established by a decision. These are often referred to as acts, actions, or strategies that are under control and are known to the decision maker.
- State of Nature: Actual events that may occur in the future, known as states of nature. At the time of the decision, the decision maker does not know and has no power over the state of nature in the future.
- Payoff: The combination of a course of action and an event is correlated with a payoff, which determines the net profit to the decision maker resulting from a combination of decisions and events.
- Payoff table: The payoff table is a way of organizing and explaining the payoffs of the various decisions, despite the specific states of nature of the decision-making problem.

The types of decisions that people make depend on the amount of knowledge or facts they have about the situation. Decision analysis is a common method that can be applied to a variety of different forms of organizational decision making:

a. Decision Making Under Uncertainty: When there are several states of nature and the manager cannot reliably assess the probabilities or if there is basically no data available on probabilities, the condition is called decision making under uncertainty:

1. Maximax (optimistic)
2. Maximin (pessimistic)
3. Hurwicz (criterion of realism)
4. Laplace (equally likely)
5. Minimax (regret)

b. Decision Making Under Risk: If the decision maker chooses a number of choices, the probability of which can be estimated, it is referred to as decision under risk. The probability of different outcomes can be objectively estimated from historical data. However, in some cases, decision makers may also be able to allocate probabilities to different outcomes on the basis of their knowledge and judgment.

1. Expected monetary value (EMV)
2. Expected opportunity loss (EOL)
3. Expected value of perfect information (EVPI)

c. Not Collective but Collaborative Intelligence: Collective intelligence aggregates input from large numbers of discrete, generally anonymous, responders to specific, generally quantitative, questions, using algorithms to process input from these responders to generate better-than-average predictions. By contrast, collaborative intelligence offers principles and frameworks to tap the diverse expertise of generally nonanonymous participants in a problem-solving process.

d. Diversity of Teams: Increasingly, organizations are learning to value diversity. Diversity can provide a powerful competitive advantage. Diversity should enhance performance by bringing more perspectives and a wider range of knowledge to bear on problems, increasing creativity, and decision-making effectiveness.

## Not HR but Talent Management

The talent or competency levels of team members significantly affects the output of the team. The term *human capital* was coined in the early 1960s by economists to encompass the knowledge embodied in individuals. However, the concept of human capital became almost undistinguishable from the proxy used to measure it, that is, formal years of education, although it was insufficient to fully account for the complexity of knowledge in individuals. Human capital is associated with two basic concepts, namely, productivity and investment. Human capital referred to the knowledge, skills, and competencies embodied in individuals that increase their productivity. These skills are acquired over one's lifetime through intergenerational transfers of knowledge, personal contacts, work experience, on-the-job-training, education, and socialization. Acquired skills represent the actualization of this potential mostly through individual efforts involving a cost. Subsequently, this concept was extended to include elements such as innate abilities, physical fitness, and healthiness, which are crucial for an individual's success in acquiring knowledge and skills. The link between human capital and investment was suggestive of the fact that it was conceived as an acquired ability rather than an innate one. In other words, nurturing mattered more than nature.

This prompted a search for a better way to assess knowledge that looked at the tasks performed by individuals in the labor market—their occupation. While knowledge measured by formal years of education is a static concept, a *store* variable that does not change over time, knowledge measured by occupation becomes a more dynamic concept, a *flow* variable. Other important elements have also been proposed as key to individual's knowledge, such as entrepreneurship, which stresses the ability of individuals in identifying and seeking opportunities for profit and taking risks that have been linked to economic growth. All such multidimensional set of individual abilities were subsumed under the collective concept of *talent*. In contrast to the human capital, the concept of *talent* is linked more to nature than nurture.

Learning is not just what happens in training courses and programs, but something that happens continually. Most of what people know and retain is from what they learn on the job through actual experience: the more they experience, the better they become. A learning organization must be one where experience is passed on and shared, and where people coach and teach each other naturally as part of their everyday routine, and one that invests seriously to improve formal learning experiences and the management of knowledge across the enterprise. In HR, in learning and development, and in knowledge management, leading organizations are targeting the specific workforces and processes that are most critical to business performance and form part of their distinctive capabilities, competencies, and skills (Bredin and Soderlund 2011).

Skills are what the individual is able to do and are developed from learning and experience. Competencies are the overall set of skills, knowledge, and behaviors needed for an individual to carry out his or her role effectively.

## Employee Engagement

Kahn (1990) was the first to say that an employee's beliefs about the organization, alignment with values and association with leaders and work processes impact how he or she is able to perform and contribute to his or her role expectations. Catering to emotional needs of employees can create a better attitude in people and also helps them to cope with any stress that is likely to appear at the workplace. Positive emotions let people think in a more open and flexible manner leading to greater creativity and energy. Thus, meeting the right combination of physical, emotional, and psychological needs of employees enables them to contribute positively to their organizations. Strong references to emotive elements like values, leadership, and culture elevated the concept of engagement from being just a state of physical involvement of an employee to that where one is emotionally involved and psychologically associated with the organization (Turner 2020; Chowdhury 2019; Gebauer and Lowman 2008).

Employee engagement is a measurement of an employee's emotional commitment to an organization; it takes into account the amount of discretionary effort an employee expends on behalf of the organization. Employee satisfaction is a measurement of an employee's *happiness* with current job and conditions; it does not measure how much effort the employee is willing to expend. Herzberg's (1964) motivation–hygiene theory articulates the higher-order psychological and emotional factors that drive them to give their best to and be committed to their workplace as against the basic requirements in an organization for one to carry out his or her job; the former is termed as motivation factors and the latter hygiene factors.

The characteristics of hygiene and motivation and hygiene factors are:

i. Motivation factors include aspects such as work challenge, recognition, responsibilities, growth prospects, learning opportunities, sense of achievement, and so on.

ii. Hygiene factors include aspects such as pay and benefits, work conditions, job security, designation, leaves and work hours, and so on.

Employee satisfaction is a stepping stone to employee engagement.
Whereas hygiene factors are the minimum required for employees to be
working in a stable and satisfying manner, motivation factors drive people
to see meaning in their work, stretch themselves, give in the extra, and
feel a connect with their organizations; in other words, they contribute
toward engagement. Hygiene factors are essential for motivation factors
to be realized.

Engaged employees are better able to navigate change and are able to better deal with uncertainty. Engaged teams display higher maturity in uncertain
situations. Knowledge sharing becomes more seamless and employees tend
to grow by sharing rather than withholding information. Collaboration, and
not competition, becomes more evident. This helps better tapping into tacit
knowledge that rests with individuals and teams. Better team bonding helps
in better alignment with organizational values and goals.

Employee engagement levels have a direct correlation to business
performance—highly engaged employees are able to contribute exponentially better than the disengaged.

## Teams and Innovation

Teams are essential to the success of startup innovation and entrepreneurship. They differ from groups, in that they have a common purpose, complementary skills, common goals, and joint accountability. Teams are also
an integral part of the management process in successful organizations.
Used effectively, teams enhance performance, quality, efficiency, and
innovation. The relationship between teams and innovation and entrepreneurship is supported by several studies that suggest that team-founded
new ventures are more successful than individually founded ventures.

Teams serve two purposes:

i. Teams create a social network of individuals with different backgrounds.
ii. Diverse teams provide an opportunity for knowledge aggregation
and integration.

## Conclusion

This chapter presented aspects of building high-performance teams, including team-based management, not HR but talent management, role-based rather than function-based responsibilities, employee engagement, team building, personnel and team performance management, and so on. Whereas a hardworking founder deeply involved in operative activities is important to survive the first years and bring his or her vision to reality, subsequently, the ability of taking over a more managerial role or pass this responsibility on to somebody specialist in the concerned field becomes essential.

*This chapter presented the aspects of building high-performance teams. This chapter highlighted a factor that is very critical for a startup: long-run consistent productive results are always delivered by the optimal effort of a team and not by a team of superhuman individuals. Also a team working together can overcome all possible encountered problems easily—there is no need for every member to have every useful ability or skill.*

# CHAPTER 10

# Skills

## Topics Covered

- Base Skills
- Data Science
  - Statistical Inference
- Intelligent Systems
  - Narrow Artificial Intelligence (Narrow AI)
    - Chatbots
  - General Artificial Intelligence (General AI)
    - Machine Learning
      - *Supervised Learning*
      - *Unsupervised Learning*
      - *Reinforcement Learning*
    - Deep Learning
    - Generative AI and OpenAI GPT-3
  - Super Artificial Intelligence (Super AI)
- Modeling and Simulation
  - Model Systems in Biology
  - Digital Twins
- Complexity
  - Systems Science
  - Design Science
- DevSecOps
  - Cloud-based Development and Deployment
  - Multitenancy

## Introduction

*This chapter presents the skills essential for productive teams of entrepreneurial ventures in the 21st century, namely, data science, intelligent systems*

*development (narrow, general, and super AI), and design thinking. It intro-*
*duces digital twins as the next level of approach to modeling and simulation.*

## Base Skills

Along with the basic knowledge requirements, employees need to develop the essential skills they need to do their jobs. The knowledge economy constantly redefines the skills it demands from the current workforce. In particular, it requires ever-greater competencies associated with information technology. Other important primary skills for every modern organization are problem-solving skills, ability to innovate, dealing with change, team working, and people management skills.

For the 21st century, organizations require a set of generic skills as described next:

1. Communications Skills: All startup employees must necessarily have basic communication skills, in listening, reading and writing, and presentation. By extension, all startup members must be comfortable with using groupware methods tools and capabilities deployed across the organization.
2. Mathematics skills: Every employee needs to master basic math skills, at least to the level of algebra. In today's world of statistical process control charts and spreadsheets, elementary understanding of algebra and statistics is mandatory for all employees.
3. Self-management skills: Employees must take responsibility for planning and managing their own careers, their own learning, and how they apply that learning to their jobs. With the advent of gig economy, employees must learn how to manage themselves and their careers so that although they may not have a guarantee of lifetime employment, they can have reasonable assurance of lifetime employability. Startups must make learning opportunities available to employees and providing pointers and access the necessary learning resources within and without the company.
4. Team Skills: Startups being constituted of a network of projects, high-performance work teams would be a prerequisite for startup excellence.

5. Function-Specific Skills: Whether in accounting, inventory, engineering, or sales, there is a set of role-specific competencies each employee must achieve to get the job done.
6. Business Skills: Employees who have spent their lives implementing decisions their managers have made to know automatically how to analyze problems and make their own decisions. All employees must learn to understand the company's basic business processes and its financial statements.

As this book is focused on high-tech startups, under function-specific skills, we will focus on contemporary software environments and related skills that are essential for high-tech startups.

## Data Science

*Data science* is the umbrella term that first appeared in 2013, encompassing statistics, data mining, data analytics, big data analytics, business intelligence (BI), AI, ML, and DL. While statistics, data science, and data analytics are often used as synonyms, there are differences between the three disciplines, most specifically in terms of knowledge and skills. Data science is a ubiquitous term designating an interdisciplinary field regarding processes and systems to gain knowledge and insights from data.

i. Statistics

When there is uncertainty, or our knowledge is imperfect, errors are inevitable. The science of statistics entails two kinds of effort: reducing the error as much as possible and ameliorating its effects, that is, managing the error (Yu 2022).

Descriptive statistics summarize the data by describing what the data look like. Descriptive statistics involve organizing a set of numbers by providing a frequency distribution and shapes of distribution for numerical data (skewed, normal), and reporting the central tendency (mean, median, or mode) and by how much scores vary from each other (as measured by range, interquartile, or standard deviation).

Correlational statistics describe relationships between two or more variables. While correlational studies do not show causality, they show preliminary information about associations among variables before causality can be determined with further analysis.

Inferential statistics help to assess the appropriateness of making inferences from a sample to a population. It is to ask: is what's true about a sample also true about the population? This involves knowledge about random sampling and the degree to which the sample does or does not represent the population.

ii. Data Mining

Data mining is so named because it is data-driven, and thus, the data miner is essentially the data explorer or data discoverer. Due to its exploratory character, data mining is also named knowledge discovery in databases (KDD). Further, because data mining often utilizes ML algorithms, many people view it as a process of data modeling by ML. Data mining is a group of nonparametric techniques for automatically extracting useful information and relationships from immense quantities of data.

iii. Big Data Analytics

In-memory analytics (IMA): The data are analyzed when they are open in the computer's random access memory (RAM), as opposed to analyzing data stored on physical disks. As the data size gets bigger and bigger, it is time-consuming to transfer the data from a database to a laptop or a server housing the analytical system. One of the viable solutions is a combination of Hadoop and MapReduce; Hadoop is a distributed file system, whereas MapReduce is a system for in-database analytics in a way that is tolerant of hardware faults due to redundancy. Hadoop is an open-source software framework for storing data and running applications on linked servers—rather than sending data back and forth, the program is executed on the server where the data are stored. MapReduce is a programming model in the Hadoop framework for accessing and analyzing big data.

## Intelligent Systems

Computers are patently lifeless objects, and they do not learn, decide, recognize, or prefer anything, at least not in the way humans do. However, lacking any standard for defining intelligence, it has been accepted as expedient to use human intelligence as the hallmark for defining intelligence. The ascription of human characteristics to inanimate objects, and also animals and plants, is referred to as anthropomorphizing. Thus, computers can be characterized by humanlike things such as discerning, learning, perceiving, understanding, and so on with the primary purpose of realizing intelligent systems. Consequently, AI systems are often associated with rational patterns of behavior that humans are capable of. While anthropomorphizing may be helpful in explaining the purpose of AI systems, it is important to remember that it is not a description of how such systems operate. The field of AI is divided broadly into the categories of narrow AI, general AI, and super AI.

### Narrow AI

Narrow AI category follows a rule-based, symbolic understanding of AI. In this view, AI is expressed in words, numbers, and other symbols that an intelligent entity can understand and manipulate. Despite significant initial promise, its performance has not been able to breakthrough the constraining barriers to surpass or even surpass human intelligence. Narrow AI (also known as weak AI) is a system that can automate tasks that are typically performed by humans but do so in a specific narrow knowledge domain. The task could be descriptive, predictive, or prescriptive and the performance of the machine can be equal to or better than that of the human (Priyadarshini et al. 2023; Kaliraj and Devi 2022).

An expert system (ES) is computer software created to solve complicated issues and offer decision-making capabilities similar to those of a human expert. This is accomplished by using both facts and heuristics, and the system retrieving information from its knowledge base in accordance with user queries, utilizing reasoning, and inference procedures. A conventional problem-solving system has both data structures and programs encoded, whereas an ES just has data structures hard-coded and does not have any problem-specific information encoded in the program. ES emulate human expert decision making through expert knowledge expressed mostly with if-then rules and decision making enabled by reasoning. Majority of ES includes a user interface and an inference engine.

These systems are created for a specific industry, like medicine, mining, and so on. Each ES shares the feature that, after being fully constructed, it will be evaluated and proved using the same real-world problem-solving scenario. However, not all ES contain learning components that allow them to adjust to new circumstances or satisfy new demands.

Narrow AI based on predefined sets of rules given by a subject matter expert is heavily focused on rule-based systems that made predictions. However, as these structures were brittle and relied on *expert advice*, they gradually fell out of use.

## Chatbots

In the year 1950, Alan Turing, an English computer scientist, put forward a question "Are machines able to think?" and he answered it by bringing the concept of Turing test. Turing test is a methodology to determine if a computer can think like a human, which marked the beginning of AI. Chatbots became a topic of research interest since the appearance of ELIZA chatbot around 1966 created by Joseph Weizenbaum and the popularization of AI as stimulated by HAL 9000 that appeared in the movie *A Space Odyssey* in 2000. In recent times, some proprietary systems have gained prestige, mostly because of the companies that have provided the platform and competition between them. Siri, Cortana, Alexa, and Google Now are intelligent personal assistant software agents developed by Apple, Microsoft, Amazon, and Google, respectively. These systems possess robust NLP and solid backend processing in order to answer direct user queries. Frequently, these systems perform intent recognition well and provide answers the user did not explicitly queried for (Galitsky 2019).

There are two different ways to attain a response from a chatbot, either by generating response from start as per ML models or by using a heuristic approach to select the most promising response from the library of predefined responses. Chatbots can generate response either by using classifiers of machine learning or by using conditional statement *if then else*:

i. In the first, the chatbot is trained to pick up a pattern of data from a training set of thousands of already existing patterns that are likely to be faced by chatbot.

ii. In the second, artificial intelligence markup language (AIML) is used in the development of the chatbot for writing patterns and response. These bots dissect user message, notice synonyms and ideas, tag components of speech, and conclude that rule matches the user question. But, these bots don't run ML algorithms or application programming interfaces (APIs) until they are programmed specially.

Chatbots have begun to resemble dialogue systems in their use of natural language understanding and generation, as well as dialogue management. For instance, the purpose of a task-oriented chatbot is to achieve a certain satisfactory goal (e.g., retrieve parameters and execute a transaction) and to do so as rapidly and accurately as practical. By contrast, nontask-oriented chatbots focus on social conversation where the goal is to interact while maintaining an appropriate level of engagement with a human interlocutor. For instance, the goal of nontask-oriented chatbots is to keep the human user engaged in the conversation for as extended period of time as possible.

Human conversations in social domain follow the structure that guides their evolution over time. This structure includes elements familiar to participating interlocutors such as conventions for engagement and disengagement, a succession of topics (with heuristics for identifying promising successors), as well as monitoring engagement level and picking strategies for managing topic transitions (for keeping track of the changing contexts).

## General AI

General AI category employs statistical methods to recognize patterns, using experience embodied in the form of digital data, repetition, and feedback loops. As this involves learning in a metaphorical sense, this approach has come to be known as ML. Using techniques such as neural networks, it is possible to construct systems that improve over time through ever more data and more powerful computers—made available and accessible through cloud computing services. The statistical approach has been yielding impressive results since 2010s. General AI (GAI) is artificial intelligence that can perform human expert tasks in multiple domains. Their performance can be equal to or even better than a human. GAI interacts with humans in a manner that humans cannot tell the difference whether they are acting with a machine or a human, that is, it passes the Turing test.

Interrelation between AI, ML, and DL is as stated as follows (Hopgood 2022):

- AI is a field of computer science focused on making computers more intelligent so that they can imitate intelligent human behavior. AI is a medium to enable computers to learn and engage in human-like thought processes, such as learning, reasoning, and self-correction. Traditionally, this involved hardcoding knowledge about the world in the form of computer programs, but success was limited because most human knowledge evolves with experiences and is subjective, intuitive, and challenging to articulate using a set of rules.
- ML enables computers to learn real-world knowledge by identifying patterns from the data and self-correction from the learning process to enable decision making. However, ML algorithms also suffer from a tradeoff as their performance is highly dependent on the how data are presented to them.
- DL algorithms solved the ingestion-dependency problem by extracting information from the input data on their own. DL as a subset of ML makes the computer learning more powerful, flexible, and abstract.

Additional details are available in the Appendix section (**A.10.1 General Artificial Intelligence (GAI)**) available online.

## Super AI

The elements of super AI are not limited to a specific scope or set of algorithms, but work intelligently in a broad range of circumstances and problem spaces. Instead of any specific technology, described next are potential and development directions in super AI:

a. Robot AI: The currently operated reactive systems define the robot's environment first, and then record its initially coded behaviors. By contrast, the envisaged robot AI is characterized by the fact that a model of the environment in which the robot operates is first created, and then a number of alternative strategies based on this model are considered to achieve a certain result. Implementation occurs for the optimal strategy from the point of view of achieving the desired outcome.

b. Quantum AI: It is based on the opportunity to use quantum computers for furthering the development of quantum AI, which will further development of AI. Quantum AI is an interdisciplinary area of activities that focuses on building quantum algorithms in order to improve computational *abilities* in the area of AI.

c. Brain Emulation: This concept assumes creating a computer program whose attributes would reflect the retention of human personality. A process consisting in copying or transferring the human consciousness to the computer.

d. Artificial Consciousness: It is an attempt to model and implement those aspects of human cognition that are identified with the idea regarding the phenomenon of brain consciousness. The phenomenon of consciousness is determined by biological, social, and cultural aspects, which renders it inextricably complicated.

e. Wetware and Biological Systems: Wetware means any equipment (hardware) or software systems (software) with a biological component (wetware), which operate as a regular computer. This is conceptually related to *artificial life*, differing from AI in that the ideas are based on fundamental biological processes and not related to intelligence or expert knowledge per se. The potential of wetware applications seem to be particularly high in such domains as bioengineering, genetic research, synthetic biology, or medical neuroengineering.

## Modeling and Simulation

Science provides the basic structure of our models used to envisage new products. It miniaturizes modules that perform a specific function that eventually leads to better materials. Understanding a real object is one thing, teaching a computer to simulate a real object is much more demanding: reality as described by a mathematical model can be optimized easily; innovation can be done on the computer. Science improves models, technology miniaturizes with equal or higher performance, and new materials and processes result. Uncertainties and risks within innovation projects can be reduced, which will lead to more routine innovations in the future.

## Model Systems in Biology

Drosophila are called fruit flies because they like to feed on the yeast that grows on fruits. Their ascension to supermodel status in biology began with the work of Thomas H. Morgan and his collaborators in the first few decades of the 20th century. Morgan had been interested in determining whether new species form by the accrual of many minor mutations, as Darwin had proposed, or by major mutations that cause large changes in the phenotype. Particularly important was that fruit flies breed year-round and rapidly, with a generation time of 10 to 20 days; each female is able to produce around 300 offspring during her lifetime. With this high reproduction rate, Morgan was able to breed tens of millions of flies, which allowed him to identify mutants even when mutation rates were relatively low. Fruit flies were also easy to feed (with bananas in the early days) and maintain as separate breeding colonies in small spaces. In addition, fruit flies tolerate extensive inbreeding better than many other species, which allowed Morgan's team to create very uniform strains in which mutants are more apparent than in heterogeneous populations.

## Digital Twins

Modeling and simulation have become the cornerstone of engineering and science for the last few decades. A large amount of research and development work has been directed toward computational methods for improving modeling. Such computer models are useful for system design and serve to mitigate the high costs of experiments and testing. However, there is a need to track the evolution of systems with time for diagnostics, prognostics, and life management (Ganguli et al. 2023). Degradation models of systems coupled with data emanating from sensors placed on the system allow the construction of digital twins, which permit tracking of a physical system in real time. The digital twin is an adaptive computer model (of the physical twin) that resides in the computer cloud.

## Complexity of Enterprises

There is no single concept of complexity (or simplicity) that is relevant for all purposes. Universal concepts of complexity are likely to be uncomputable in practice and, on the other hand, practical concepts of complexity are likely to be applicable to very narrow class of systems. The uncomputability of complexity can be traced back to the impossibility of finding optimal descriptions of a system. Complexity is always understood in the context of a level of abstraction of the system, which, in turn, is dependent on:

- Amount of information the design embodies
- Amount of information that is rendered irrelevant

### Systems Science

A system is defined as a set of elements that have one or more relationships between them, and systems thinking is the process by which one seeks to understand those elements and relationships so as to be able to understand the behavior of the system as a whole. Systems are usually visualized graphically as a set of nodes with links or connections between them. A system is more than the sum of its parts, particularly if it is large or complex. It may exhibit unique behavior that cannot necessarily be inferred from the behavior of its individual elements or any subset of them. In systems theory, it is important to have perspective, as a very small observer of a single element may be oblivious to larger interactions that might be clear to a giant observer of the entire system (Chowdhury 2019).

Additional details are available in the Appendix section (**A.10.2 System Science**) available online.

### Design Science

The importance of innovation as a means of solving the problems of an increasingly complex society is growing. Design thinking is a method used to realize innovation in the technology as well as business domains using a human-centered approach with a designer's thinking and aesthetics (Johannesson and Perjons 2021; Wieringa 2014).

Traditionally, the two diametrically opposing approaches to problem-solving can be categorized as:

- Deductive
- Inductive

Design thinking weaves these two opposing methods together into abductive reasoning. Design thinking uses abductive reasoning to infer ever-improving solutions, up to the point where the outcome is considered good enough or can no longer be improved upon. The abductive reasoning framework starts with observations to seek a first-cut simple and intuitive solution. Oftentimes, the initial solution is either only a partial solution or only partially addresses the problem at hand. Often, the initial solution results in a rephrased problem statement. By subsequently analyzing the intuitive solution and gathering data to either validate or invalidate it, the initial solution is revised and improved upon.

Additional details are available in the Appendix section (**A.10.3 Design Science**) available online.

# DevSecOps

Developer security operations (DevSecOps) is just a process for software development methodology whose emphasis is on collaboration, communication, automation, integration, and a means how the cooperation between the IT systems, security and operations professional, and the software developers can be measured. In this method of software development, there is interdependency between the members of the software development team. It is due to this the development team finds it possible to develop and deliver software rapidly and improve the performance of the various operations (Wilson 2020).

Operations responsibilities range from supporting deployed applications to enforcing organizationwide security rules. DevSecOps involves the modifications of both Dev and Ops practices: operations personnel may need to be trained in the types of runtime errors that can occur in a system under development; they may have suggestions as to the type and structure of log files; and they may provide other types of input into the requirements process. At the other end, developers may need to be made more responsible for monitoring the progress and errors that occur during deployment and execution, so theirs would be the inputs suggesting the primary requirements.

While the automation of the deployment pipeline is an important component, DevSecOps is based on the following principles:

- The principles of flow, which mainly address the fast delivery of work from development to operation
- The principles of feedback, which add feedback of information about problems in operations back to development
- The principles of continual learning and experimentation

DevSecOps involves broadly the following aspects:

1. DevSecOps enforces a deployment process to be used by all, including Dev, Sec, and Ops personnel, to ensure a higher quality of deployments. This avoids errors caused by ad hoc deployments and the resulting misconfiguration, as well as optimizes the time it takes to diagnose and repair an error. The normal deployment process should make it easy to trace the history of a particular deployment artifact and understand the components that were included in that artifact.

2. DevSecOps uses continuous deployment to shorten the time between a developer committing code to a repository and the code being deployed. Continuous deployment also emphasizes automated tests to increase the quality of code making its way into production.

3. DevSecOps enforces development of infrastructure code, such as deployment scripts, with the same set of practices as application

code to ensure both high quality in the deployed applications and deployments proceeding as per plan. Errors in deployment scripts such as misconfigurations can cause errors in the application, the environment, or the deployment process. Applying quality control practices used in normal software development to the development of operations scripts and processes will help in controlling the quality of these specifications.

### Cloud-Based Development and Deployment

As indicated earlier, with the advancement in computing technologies, including cloud computing, distributed computing, blockchain, and IoT, the existing frameworks and management approaches do not apply satisfactorily. This has given rise to the requirement for software to be scalable, sustainable, and suitable for distributed computing environments. In turn, this suggests a major requirement for cloud-based application development methods with evolutionary lifecycles and corresponding deployment approaches.

Figure 10.1 shows a comparison between the traditional software development lifecycle (SDLC) and a contemporary cloud-based software development lifecycle (CDLC).

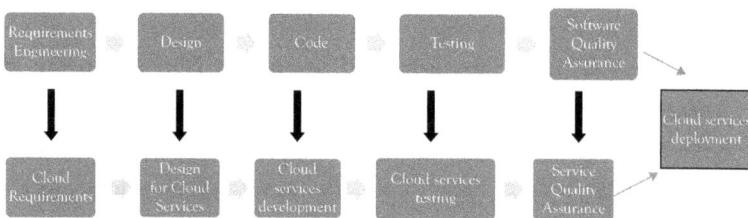

*Figure 10.1 Traditional SDLC versus CDLC*

### Multitenancy

Multitenancy is the single most important attribute of software-as-a-service (SaaS) in any cloud solution. Multitenancy, in a generic sense, refers to many tenants residing in the same house simultaneously and paying rent in proportion to their period of stay, or to the extent of use of various facilities. Multitenancy, in the context of SaaS in cloud software, refers to any software's ability to serve multiple enterprises simultaneously. *Tenants* in this context refer to customer enterprises using the SaaS in cloud model. In essence, multitenancy refers to many customer enterprises that simultaneously use the same running instance of software—each customer enterprise pays a fee as rent based on the duration of their usage of selected facilities or functionalities in the SaaS solutions or products.

This demands a new architecting approach for tackling requirements such as multitenant customization and extensibility, data scaling, and isolation. To make a single instance of software serve multiple tenants, various tiers and components of the software should have been architected differently. Each component needs to be designed suitably to achieve this characteristic. For example, the web tier would require customization of user screens through metadata. Similarly, the data tier would require providing the right data model—either a dedicated DB for each tenant or one DB for tenants (permitting customization).

## Conclusion

This chapter presented an overview of the skills essential for productive teams of entrepreneurial ventures in the 21st century, namely, data science, intelligent systems development (AI/ML/DL), and design thinking. The field of AI is subdivided into narrow AI, general AI, and super AI. Narrow AI category follows a rule-based, symbolic understanding of AI; it is based on advice of experts embodied into a predefined sets of rules, which are then queried upon. Examples of narrow AI include currently popular chatbots like OpenAI GPT-3.

General AI category employs statistical methods to recognize patterns, using experience embodied in the form of digital data, repetition, and feedback loops. As this involves learning in a metaphorical sense, this approach has come to be known as machine learning (ML). The three main techniques for learning are learning by example, learning by exploration, and learning by trial and error, and are, respectively, called as supervised, unsupervised, and reinforcement learning. Reinforcement learning or trial-and-error-based learning method is based on giving rewards for the desired behaviors and punishments for the undesired ones. Deep learning corresponds to those tasks that humans solve intuitively, such as speech or face recognition, but whose solution is difficult to formulate through mathematical rules. A computer-based solution for this type of task involves the ability of computers to learn from experience and to understand the world in terms of a hierarchy of concepts—each concept is defined by its relationship to simpler concepts. The hierarchy of concepts allows the computer to learn complicated concepts by assembling them from simpler ones. Hence, the name *deep learning*.

General AI category employs statistical methods to recognize patterns, using experience embodied in the form of digital data, repetition, and feedback loops. As this involves learning in a metaphorical sense, this approach has come to be known as ML. Super AI is not limited to a specific scope or set of algorithms but demonstrates human-surpassing intelligence in a broad range of circumstances and problem spaces. This seems likely to be unachievable in a foreseeable future. Design thinking is a method used to realize innovation in the technology as well as business domains using a human-centered approach with a designer's thinking and aesthetics.

*This chapter presented the skills essential for productive teams of entrepreneurial ventures in the 21st century, namely, data science, intelligent systems development (narrow, general, and super AI), and design thinking. It introduced digital twins as the next level of approach to modeling and simulation.*

# CHAPTER 11

# Systems

## Topics Covered

- Business Operating Environment
- Network Systems
  - WWW
  - Social Networks
  - Sensor Networks
- Platform Systems
  - Internet of Things (IoT)
- Ecosystems
  - Bio
  - Nano
  - Industry 4.0

## Introduction

*This chapter presents the details on currently available foundational systems like sensor networks, IoT, and Industry 4.0 (also termed as Industrial IoT (IIoT) in the United States) that are essential for any startup of the 21st century. It highlights how the transition from internally focused to network-, platform-, and ecosystem-centric ways of working brings with it many practical advantages. It allows for companies to focus on their core competencies and to progressively outsource all activities that are not strategic to the company.*

## Business Operating Environment

In most traditional organizations, the business operating environment (BOE) follows a sequential and centrally directed formula, which promotes rational decision making. It can be characterized as focused on individualistic choice behavior; information-led rather than intelligence-led where information is sought to reduce uncertainty and justify the decision-making process. This classic BOE, or series of decision-making algorithms, has remained unchanged since the last century, despite valiant attempts from the 1970s onward to move away from transactional to transformational leadership—away from leading through coercion and conditioning to cultivating followership.

The new BOE that departs from linearity and is fit for purpose for Industry 4.0 and the new economy. BOE 2.0 is a complex adaptive system (CAS) that makes collective sense of organizational intelligence using agreed criteria and simple algorithms that are processed through interconnected, self-organizing, sensemaking networks. Here, collaborative decisions emerge through collaboration, optimization, feedback loops, and group consensus or swarm.

BOE 2.0 is a CAS; complex implies diversity—a great number of connections between a wide variety of elements; adaptive suggests the capacity to alter or change—the ability to learn from experience; system is a set of connected or interdependent things (see Chapter 10, *Systems Science* subsection). A CAS has a densely connected web of interacting agents each operating from their own schema or local knowledge. Thus, CAS embraces a broad group of disciplines, building on the work carried out in fields such as complexity science, chaos theory, biology, computer science, systems theory, AI, and game theory.

## Network Systems

At its most basic level, a network system is any system or structure of interconnected elements that can be represented by a graph of nodes (the elements) connected by some kind of links (whatever ties them together). The nodes of a network may be anything from landmasses to cells in a body, political institutions, or people. The links between the nodes might be physical connections, biochemical interactions, relationships of power and authority, or reciprocal social ties such as friendship.

### World Wide Web

The World Wide Web (WWW) was invented by Tim Berners-Lee in 1990 at CERN in Geneva, Switzerland. The invention of the WWW by

Berners-Lee was a revolution in the use of the Internet. Users could now surf the Web: that is, hyperlink among the millions of computers in the world and obtain information easily. The WWW creates a space in which users can access information easily in any part of the world. This is done using only a web browser and simple web addresses. Browsers are used to connect to remote computers over the Internet and to request, retrieve, and display the web pages on the local machine. The user can then click on hyperlinks on web pages to access further relevant information that may be on an entirely different continent. Berners-Lee developed the first web browser called the WorldWideWeb browser. He also wrote the first browser program, and this allowed users to access web pages throughout the world. The invention of the WWW was announced in August 1991, and the growth of the Web has been phenomenal since then.

## Social Networks

Decades before the arrival of websites like Facebook, sociologists attempted to map the social ties within groups via the field of social network analysis (SNA). The defining feature of SNA is its focus on the structure of relationships, ranging from casual acquaintance to close bonds. SNA maps and measures the formal and informal relationships to understand what facilitates or impedes the knowledge flows that bind the interacting units (Roy and Zeng 2015). SNA is focused on uncovering the patterning of people's interaction. The social network analysts believe that how an individual lives depends in large part on how that individual is tied into the larger web of social connections.

Nodes are the individuals or groups involved in the network, and links are connections, or ties, between individuals or groups. A nodes importance in a social network refers to its centrality. Central nodes have the potential to exert influence over less central nodes. A network that possesses just a few or perhaps even one node with high centrality is a centralized network. In this type of network, all nodes are directly connected to each other. Subordinate nodes direct information to the central node, and the central node distributes it to all other nodes. Centralized networks are susceptible to disruption because they have few central nodes, and damage to a central node could be devastating to the entire network. Decentralized networks are those that do not possess one central hub but rather possess several important hubs. Each node is indirectly tied to all others, and therefore, the network has more elasticity. Consequently, these networks are more difficult to disrupt due to their loose connections and ability to replace damaged nodes.

The term degrees is used in reference to the number of direct connections that a node enjoys—the node that possesses the largest number of connections is the *hub of the network*. The term betweenness refers to the number of groups that a node is indirectly tied to through the direct links that it possesses. Therefore, nodes with high a degree of betweenness act as liaisons or bridges to other nodes in the structure. These nodes are known as *brokers* because of the power that they wield. However, these *brokers* represent a single point of failure because if their communication flows is disrupted than they will be cut off to the nodes that it connects. Closeness measures the trail that a node would take in order to reach all other nodes in a network. A node with high closeness does not necessarily have the most direct connections, but because they are *close* to many members, they maintain rapid access to most other nodes through both direct and indirect ties.

### Sensor Networks

A sensor network consists of a large number of sensor nodes that are densely deployed in a sensing region and collaborate to accomplish a sensing task (Fahmy 2016). It requires a suite of network protocols to implement various network control and management functions, for example, synchronization, self-configuration, medium access control, routing, data aggregation, node localization, and network security. However, existing network protocols for traditional wireless networks, for example, cellular systems and mobile ad hoc networks (MANETs), cannot be applied directly to sensor networks because they do not consider the energy, computation, and storage constraints in sensor nodes. Enabled by recent advances in microelectronic mechanical systems (MEMS) and wireless communication technologies, tiny, cheap, and smart sensors deployed in a physical area and networked through wireless links and the Internet, wireless sensor networks (WSNs) provide unprecedented opportunities for a variety of applications like industry process control and environmental monitoring.

In contrast with the traditional wireless communication networks like cellular systems and MANET, there are many challenges in the development and application of WSNs because of many have unique characteristics:

- Application-Specific: Sensor networks are application-specific. A network is usually designed and deployed for a specific application. The design requirements of a network change with its application.
- No Global Identification: Due to the large number of sensor nodes, it is usually not possible to build a global addressing scheme for a sensor network because it would introduce a high overhead for the identification maintenance.
- Frequent Topology Change: Network topology changes frequently due to node failure, damage, addition, energy depletion, or channel fading.
- Dense Node Deployment: Sensor nodes are usually densely deployed in a field of interest. The number of sensor nodes in a sensor network can be several orders of magnitude higher than that in a MANET.
- Many-to-One Traffic Pattern: In most sensor network applications, the data sensed by sensor nodes flow from multiple source sensor nodes to a particular sink, exhibiting a many-to-one traffic pattern.
- Battery-Powered Sensor Nodes: Sensor nodes are usually powered by battery. In most situations, they are deployed in a harsh or hostile environment, where it is very difficult or even impossible to change or recharge the batteries.
- Severe Energy, Computation, and Storage Constraints: Sensor nodes are highly limited in energy, computation, and storage capacities.
- Self-Configurable: Sensor nodes are usually randomly deployed without careful planning and engineering. Once deployed, sensor nodes have to autonomously configure themselves into a communication network.

- Unreliable Sensor Nodes: Sensor nodes are usually deployed in harsh or hostile environments and operate without attendance. They are prone to physical damages or failures.
- Data Redundancy: In most sensor network applications, sensor nodes are densely deployed in a region of interest and collaborate to accomplish a common sensing task. Thus, the data sensed by multiple sensor nodes typically have a certain level of correlation or redundancy.

## Platform Systems

A platform system is defined by the subset of components used in common across a suite of products that also exhibit network effects. Network effects are demand-side economies of scale such that the value to existing consumers rises in the number of subsequent consumers (Belleflamme and Peitz 2021). Network effects are distinct from supply-side economies of scale that come from high fixed/low marginal costs, as in the case of semiconductor manufacture, where average costs decline as production volume increases. Scale economies for both demand and supply commonly occur in high technology sector but must be conceived of and managed differently. Same-side network effects refer to effects of one user group upon other members of the same group, for example, the positive network effects that PC gamers enjoy from additional users of the same game, or the negative effect on drivers of congestion on a highway. Cross-side network effects refer to demand economics of scale from one network group to another (e.g., from users to developers); for example, the effect of doctors and patients who both want to affiliate via the same Health Maintenance Organization (HMO) (Guillen 2021).

Value is exchanged among a triangular set of relationships, including consumer/user providers, component suppliers (codevelopers), and platform sponsor firms. The focus is on platforms where users experience network effects to emphasize the mutually reinforcing interests of participants in the platform system. A platform's sponsor and provider roles can be fulfilled by the same company or shared by multiple firms. Examples of platforms with a sole sponsor include Apple's Macintosh and the American Express credit card. Occasionally, however, a sole sponsor licenses multiple providers. For example, American Express granted third-party banks such as MBNA permission to issue American Express-branded credit cards. Alternatively, multiple parties may jointly sponsor a platform, typically under the auspices of an association (e.g., VISA, which is controlled by 21,000 member banks).

At the provider level, platforms are either proprietary or shared. With a proprietary platform, a single firm serves as platform provider (e.g., Monster.com, Xbox). Rival platforms employ incompatible technologies (e.g., PlayStation versus Xbox, VISA versus American Express). With a shared platform, multiple firms serve as rival providers of a common platform (e.g., VISA's issuing and acquiring banks, who support cardholders and merchants, respectively). Rival providers of a shared platform employ compatible technologies; any network user could switch providers (e.g., from a Dell PC to a Compaq PC in the case of Microsoft's Windows platform) and still interact with the same partners as before (i.e., all Windows-compatible applications). At the sponsor level, sole sponsors usually operate proprietary platforms (e.g., eBay, Apple Macintosh), whereas joint sponsorship usually leads to a shared platform (e.g., Linux, VISA).

## IoT

It is quite likely that sooner or later, the majority of items connected to the Internet will not be humans, but things. Just like the Internet and Web connects humans, the IoT connects everyday things for which IoT offers a virtual presence on the Internet, allocates a specific identity and virtual address, and adds capabilities to self-organize and communicate with other things without human intervention. IoT will primarily expand communication from the seven billion people around the world to the estimated 50 to 70 billion machines. This would result in a world where everything is connected and can be accessed from anywhere—this has a potential of connecting 100 trillion things that are deemed to exist on Earth. The increasing volume, variety, velocity, and veracity of data produced by the IoT will continue to fuel the explosion of data for the foreseeable future. With estimates ranging from 16 to 50 billion Internet connected devices by 2025, the hardest challenge for largescale, context-aware applications and smart environments is to tap into such disparate and ever-growing data streams originating from everyday devices, and to extract hidden but relevant information and hard-to-detect behavioral patterns out of it.

With the advent of IoT, the physical world itself will become a connected information system. In the world of the IoT, sensors and actuators embedded in physical objects are linked through wired and wireless networks that connect the Internet (Rayes and Salam 2022; Kagermann, Wahlster, and Helbig. 2013). This information system churns out huge volumes of data that flows to computers for analysis. When objects can both sense the environment and communicate, they become tools for understanding the complexity of the real world and responding to it swiftly. To reap the full benefits, any successful solution to build context-aware data-intensive applications, and services must be able to make this information transparent and available at a much higher frequency to substantially improve the decision making and prediction capabilities of the applications and services.

Additional details are available in the Appendix section (**A.11.1 Internet of Things (IoT) Enabling Technologies**) available online.

> It is important to highlight that this book does not discuss other foundational technologies like big data, analytics, cloud computing, mobile computing, and so on. This is not in any way indicative of their lesser significance. On the contrary, they are important prerequisites for all the concepts, technologies, and aspects discussed in this book (Kale 2019).

## Ecosystems

The transition from internally focused to ecosystem-centric ways of working brings with it many advantages. It allows for companies to focus on their core competencies, to outsource all activities that are not strategic for the company, and to employ ecosystems of third-party developers to complement the core functionality provided by the company itself with extensions for specific customer segments and customers (Gratacap et al. 2018).

Important characteristics of business ecosystems are:

i.  Symbiotic Relationships: The organizations in the ecosystem have a symbiotic relationship with each other.

ii. Coevolution: The ecosystem as a whole evolves and because of the symbiotic relationship, the organizations in the ecosystem evolve together.

iii. Platform: The organizations in the ecosystem preferably share a business platform (of services, tools, and technologies).

Instead of acting as a standalone company toward a customer base, there are many benefits of operating in an ecosystem:

a. The ecosystem provides an increased *stickiness* for existing customers. Because of the complementors and integrators, just switching away from the basic platform provided by the focal firm requires the customer overcoming a big hurdle as the solution is not as standardized as third-party solutions available in the market.

b. The ability of ecosystem partners to share the cost of innovation across the whole customer base.

c. The ecosystem can often provide a more attractive offering for new customers because of the wide range of functionality provided.

Software ecosystems like Industry 4.0 are an instance of the business ecosystem concept (like bio, nano, cogno, info) and the constituting business platform translates to a software platform like cyberphysical systems (CPS) or IoT. Typically provided by the focal firm, the software platform provides the generic functionality in the domain that is required by most of the customers. Complementors provide solutions on top of the platform and use interfaces furnished by the platform organization. Once introduced, the functionality evolves and matures progressively to become broadly adopted in the ecosystem and a differentiator for the concerned complementor to drive its business growth.

### Bio

Bioinformatics refers to informatics techniques being applied to biological problems for finding solutions. Bioinformatics is an interdisciplinary area of research that integrates biology with information technology, computer science, mathematics, statistics, physics, and chemistry.

The first bioinformatics project was the Human Genome Project in 1990, which had the goal of sequencing and annotation of the human genome. There are a number of ongoing projects in various areas of bioinformatics like sequence analysis, genomics, structural bioinformatics, and computational evolutionary biology (Byrant, Atherton, and Collins 2007).

Bioinformatics is based on the foundation of DNA, RNA, and proteins. Organisms have cells that communicate and interact to form tissues, organs, and organisms. Cells are made of membranes, proteins, carbohydrates, vitamins, and nucleic acids. Bunches of cells form tissue. Lots of tissues form an organ and organs make a whole organism. DNA is present inside the nucleus of cell. It is the cookbook for manufacturing proteins. DNA is converted to RNA before being transformed to protein(s), which are the building blocks of life.

There are three types of proteins:

i. Fibrous Proteins: These proteins form muscles fiber, connective tissue, and bone. For example, keratin, actin, myosin, collagen, and so on.

ii. Globular Proteins: These proteins carry out functions like transportation, catalyzing, and regulation. For example, hemoglobin, globulin, thrombin, and so on.

iii. Membrane Proteins: These proteins have multiple roles like connecting cells with each other, receptor proteins, and transporting molecules. For example, histones, glucose transporter, and so on.

Molecular biology is the biology of molecules like RNA, DNA, and protein, which actively participate in the processes called transcription and translation. The central dogma of molecular biology refers to the collective process of transcription, followed by translation, often called gene expression. The process starts with a double-stranded DNA, replicates itself into two single-stranded DNA, which then convert into mRNA (messenger RNA). This process is called transcription. The bases or alphabets in mRNA are grouped together in sets of three called codons. Each codon corresponds to a particular amino acid. tRNA (transfer RNA) translates these codons and transfers a free amino acid to the target place where codon and amino acid bind together in the ribosome. Sequences of amino acids form polypeptide chains and thus proteins. Ribosomes then deliver the protein into the cell. These proteins are the building blocks of our body and are responsible for all the functions in our body.

There are more than 25,000 genes within the human genome; each gene can produce more than one protein product. Accordingly, the total number of proteins in the human proteome is estimated to be more than one million. Protein–protein interaction leads to chemical reactions in our body that catalyze metabolism. The journey from genotype to phenotype is characterized by genomics and proteomics. Genotype refers to all genetic material inside our body, and phenotype refers to how we look on the outside of our body.

i. Genomics is the study of genes in the genome. The entire genetic content or DNA of an organism is called genome. In any cell, there are approximately 3.5 billion base pairs that are formed from four bases of DNA (A, C, G, T). Massively coiled DNA exists in the form of chromosomes; there are 23 chromosomes in our body.
   Genomics deals with:
   • Provide a comprehensive list of genes for the whole organism
   • Study DNA sequences and its mutations
   • Decipher the function of an DNA sequence, often called functional genomics
   • Study the flow of information within a cell
   • Diagnose new diseases and their possible treatments
   • Detect diseases in the body
   • Predict behavioral status based on gene expression
   • Figure out how to resist diseases
   • Genetically modify food
ii. Proteomics is the qualitative and quantitative study of proteomes of cellular organisms. A collection of proteins in a cell is referred to as a proteome. Each gene can produce more than one protein product. The total number of proteins in the human proteome is estimated to be more than one million. Proteomics deals with the study of the interaction of RNA, DNA, and proteins. It leads to understanding cells, which are the units of life.

Proteomics deals with:
- Identification of the structure of proteins
- Protein function
- Protein expression
- Protein localization
- Protein posttranslational modification
- Protein–protein interaction

## Nano

Nanotechnology is the science and technology of objects in the nanoscale, whose properties differ significantly from that of their constituent material at the macroscopic or even microscopic scale (Sanders 2019). The major interest in nanoparticles has been generated in the research and the industry sector mostly due to its physical and chemical properties, which differ quite a lot from the bulk (large scale) materials.

The two aspects that explain what exactly makes the nanomaterials behave differently are:

1. Surface-to-Volume (S/V) Ratio: What makes a nanomaterial special is that with increasing S/V more and more atoms/molecules of the material become exposed to the surroundings and a larger number of the so-called *dangling bonds* become available at the surface, thus making the particle more active chemically.

   The S/V ratio is simply the surface area of an object divided by its volume. For symmetrical objects like a spherical particle, this ratio is inversely proportional to the radius, and for a cube, it is inversely proportional to its sides. For a very simple example, a spherical particle of approximately 100 nm diameter has only a very small percentage approximately 2 percent of its total constituent atoms exposed to the surface, if we go down to particle diameters of approximately 3 nm, 45 to 60 percent of the atoms become exposed to the surroundings. In such circumstances, the behavior of the particle becomes altered in terms of its chemical activity.

2. Quantum Confinement: This concept arises from the size reduction of material, leading to the electronic wave functions being more tightly confined and resulting in changes associated with electronic

and optical properties of the nanomaterial. A smaller (or bigger) particle size results in a stronger (or weaker) confinement, which gives rise to enhancement (or decrease) of the band gap and modifies the band structure of the material. This results in changes in the electron mobility and effective mass, relative dielectric constant, optical properties, and so on. Metallic nanoparticles show interesting properties like variations in color of colloidal suspensions with changing particle size, UV photoemission, enhanced photoluminescence, and so on by reason of quantum confinement effect.

Nanotechnology has become an exciting area because scientists and engineers today possess a grand ability of significantly alter materials properties by proper size reduction and clever utilization of quantum confinement. The commercial applications of nanotechnology are truly diverse. Nanotech products are finding their way into a variety of different industries such as automobile, aerospace, biotechnology, cosmetics, defense, energy, electronics, health care, sports/fitness, textiles, footwear, and so on. In the aerospace industry, carbon-fiber composites for modern aircraft and helicopters help decrease weight and enhance fuel efficiency. Also, the carbon-fiber composites help decrease the RADAR profile of combat aircrafts. Shape-shifting aerofoils and winglets in future aircrafts/ space shuttles for extreme maneuverability and handling is also a topic of R&D in the aerospace industry.

### Industry 4.0

Until the last few decades, the business of the global economy was, essentially, manufacturing. The focus on goods rather than services led to a product-focused, mass market marketing strategy, resulting in a high cost of acquiring new customers, and a low cost for customers switching to other brands. There has always been a focus on customer needs, but with the advent of computers, there has been a shift away from producing goods or providing services, toward discovering and meeting the needs of the individual customer (Misra et al. 2021). Don Peppers and Martha Rogers pioneered the concept of one-to-one marketing made possible by the advent of computer-assisted database marketing. Businesses with highly diversified customer needs and highly differentiated customer valuations were expected to benefit from one-to-one customized marketing. This paradigm of one-to-one marketing has been further extended inward onto the production systems via Industry 4.0.

In the 18th century, the First Industrial Revolution, Industry 1.0, was characterized by mechanical production powered by water and steam. The industrial revolution in the 20th century, Industry 2.0, introduced mass production, based on the division of labor and powered by electrical energy. In the 1970s, Industry 3.0 was set in motion by embedded electronics and information technology (IT) for further automation of production. Industry 4.0 (especially in Europe; Industrial Internet in the United States) reflects the rise of a basket of new digitally enabled industrial technologies, that is, digital manufacturing that enable realization of the manufacturing of individual products in a batch size of one while maintaining the economic conditions of mass production, that is, mass customization.

### Industry 4.0 Principles

The Industry 4.0 principles are as follows:

1. Agility means the flexibility of the system to changing requirements by replacing or improving separated modules based on standardized software and hardware interfaces.
2. Integrated business processes are the link between physical systems and software platforms by enabling communication and coordination mechanism assisted by corporate data management services and connected networks.
3. Virtualization enables monitoring of entire system, new system adaptation, and system changes using simulation tools or augmented reality (AR).
4. Decentralization including self-decision making of the machines and relying on the learning from the previous events and actions.
5. Interoperability implies the communication of cyber physical systems (CPS) components with each other using industrial Internet and regular standardization processes to create a smart factory.

6. Service orientation is the satisfaction of customer requirements adaptation to entire system while using a perspective of integrating both internal and external subsystems.

7. Real-Time Data Management: Real-time data management is the tracing and tracking the system by online monitoring to prevent system lacks when a failure appears.

Additional details are available in the Appendix section (**A.11.2 Industry 4.0 Enabling Technologies**) available online.

# Conclusion

Systems are the surrounding environment or the context with reference to a startup, and it customarily consists of a network or platform or ecosystems or even a combination of the three. The transition from internally focused to such external-centric ways of working brings with it many advantages. It allows for companies to focus on their core competencies, and to outsource all activities that are not strategic for the company and to employ network or platform or ecosystems of third-party developers to complement the core functionality provided by the company itself with extensions targeted at specific customer segments and customers.

Instead of acting as a standalone company toward a customer base, there are many benefits of operating with such external *systems* because:

- They provide an increased *stickiness* for existing customers. Because of the complementors and integrators, just switching away from the basic systems provided by the focal firm requires the customer overcoming a big hurdle as the solution is not as standardized as third-party solutions available in the market.
- They provide the ability of *systems* partners to share the cost of innovation across the whole customer base.
- They provide a more attractive offering for new customers because of the wider range of collective functionality on offer.

*This chapter presented the details on currently available foundational systems like sensor networks, IoT, and Industry 4.0 (also termed as IIoT in the*

*United States) that are essential for any startup of the 21st century. It high-
lighted how the transition from internally focused to network-, platform-, and
ecosystem-centric ways of working brings with it many practical advantages.
It allows for companies to focus on their core competencies and to progressively
outsource all activities that are not strategic to the company.*

# CHAPTER 12

# Security

## Topics Covered

- Governance
  - ○ Digital Governance
  - ○ Governance Networks
  - ○ Blockchain
    - *Decentralized Accounting*
    - *Decentralized Finance (DeFi)*
- Identity
- Trust
- Privacy
- Security
  - ○ IoT Security Framework
- Blockchain Technology
  - ○ Features of Blockchain
  - ○ Characteristics of Blockchain
  - ○ Supply Chain Management (SCM) with Blockchain

## Introduction

*This chapter describes the critical issues of governance, identity, trust, privacy, and security. It then introduces blockchain as the panacea for addressing all these constellation of requirements. It highlights how the decentralized aspects of blockchain give rise to unique solutions like triple-entry accounting (TEA) and decentralized finance (DeFi).*

## Governance

Corporate governance is concerned with the set of practices and processes used to direct an organization (Ebert et al. 2020). It covers a broad scope, including environmental awareness, strategy, and ethical behavior. Corporate governance serves to balance the need to achieve economic goals without sacrificing social and/or environmental goals. A key challenge is to optimize the tradeoff between performance and compliance. While excessive controls hinder progress, a lack of restrictions would lead to statutory breaches and financial losses. The board of directors is charged with the responsibility of creating and preserving wealth for the stakeholders while ensuring transparency, accountability, and security. Together with executive management, they help to set up decision rights and accountability and establish governance policies aligned to business objectives. The organization then closely monitors investment returns and risks in accordance with the guidelines set.

Digital governance involves the leadership, organizational structures, and processes that enable IT to meet the organization's strategies and objectives. The organization must be able to run a robust IT operation along with key digital governance practices, such as digital portfolio management, risk management, performance management, and data governance in place. With greater clarity of the digital governance structure, roles, and processes, the organization would be able to make faster decisions and move quicker in the market.

## Digital Governance

Digital governance, as a subset of corporate governance, involves the creation and monitoring of policies for investments in and use of digital technologies across the organization. Digital governance enables collecting, using, and sharing of data and information that are organizational assets on par with money, materials, and manpower. Such intangible assets can also become valuable intellectual copyright (IC) in its own right. Digital governance is wider than IT governance. Startups must engage closely with digital technology and treat it as central to their governance activities, just as they treat issues such as cash flow, talent management, and corporate reputation (Green and Daniels 2020).

IT governance can be defined as the processes that ensure efficient and effective ways of using IT in enabling an organization to achieve its goals. All organizations use digital technology to communicate with their stakeholders, manage their operational processes, and manage and transfer money. The nature and scale of emerging risks around the use of digital technologies in business including security, privacy, and trust represent a real threat to organizational success, if not survival itself.

Digital governance enables:

- Good enforcement of regulations relating to safety at work, privacy, HR, marketing, finance, and so on that otherwise they may not be able to do so.
- Good customer service, protects privacy, prevents fraud, protects a positive organizational reputation and so on; all these in turn, collectively enhance customer trust.
- Good cybersecurity that allows organizations to take risks that otherwise they may not be in a position to do so.
- Good communication and interconnectedness that allows them to be engaged with partner companies that otherwise they may not be in a position to do so.
- Good analysis of data and information coupled with powerful technologies like AI and ML that allows them to deploy effective strategies that otherwise they may not be in a position to do so.
- Good skills assimilation that the organization needs from their employees that otherwise they may not be able to do so.

### Governance Networks

Collaborations among network actors are important, as they can affect the effectiveness of the network. In governance networks, the *nodes* (actors) are the organizations involved in networks. They measure the *network positions* of the organizations in terms of their *degree centralities* and *betweenness centralities*, both of which are social network analysis (SNA) measures that indicate how *central* a node is within a network. Degree centrality measures the number of connections a node has and betweenness centrality measures the extent to which the organization is *in-between* others. Degree centrality is the measure of *how many friends a node (an individual or organization) has,* and betweenness centrality is the measure of the *gatekeeping* role of the node. Gatekeepers can control the flow of information in a network—more connected and gatekeeping organizations are more likely to collaborate in a governance network. Organization's degree and betweenness centralities are significant predictors of their tendencies to collaborate with the other organizations in networks. And, between degree and centrality, the latter is a better predictor between the two (Morcol 2023).

In governance networks, the relations between the micro and macro levels in networks are also significant. The term micro refers to the individuals and organizations or organizational units within a governance network, while the term macro refers to the network as a whole. Degree and betweenness centralities (both of which are micro-level measures) can be measured only in relation to the whole of the network (macro level). In other words, how central focal actor in a network is depends on the size and structure of the network the focal actor is embedded. Micro-level studies have helped answer questions like:

- What are the impacts of network ties among individual actors on organizational performance?
- Which positions in organizational networks are most influential?
- How individuals in these positions within networks respond to changes within and outside the network?

Macro-level empirical studies are more difficult to conduct, and many studies at this level have remained conceptual. Macro-level studies reveal typologies that illustrate the efforts to find common patterns in governance networks and generalize about their structures.

### Blockchain

A blockchain is a database or *ledger*, that is, a continuously updated record of transactions (reflecting *who holds what* at a particular point in time). Once a transaction is verified and validated according to predefined rules and protocols, a *block* is added to the chain with all previous records in linear and chronological order. What makes the blockchain *immutable* is that the ledger or database is distributed to a countless number of participants (*nodes*) around the world in public peer-to-peer (P2P) networks (like the Internet). The distributed character of the ledger ensures that everyone trusts the blockchain to be the 'singular version truth' forever. The use of cryptographic hashes makes tampering with blockchain records very difficult. Cryptographic hashes comprise complex algorithms that would result in a different hash value upon even a minuscule change to the blockchain, making manipulation instantly and readily detectable by anyone in possession of a copy of the ledger.

Decentralized Accounting

Double-entry accounting (DEA) is a system so named because every entry to an account (debit) requires a corresponding and opposite entry to a different account (credit). If the accounting entries are recorded without error, the aggregate balance of all accounts having debit balances will be equal to the aggregate balance of all accounts having credit balances. Accounting entries that debit and credit related accounts typically include the same date and identifying code in both accounts so that in case of error, each debit and credit can be traced back to a journal and transaction source document, thus preserving an audit trail. The accounting entries are recorded in the *Books of Accounts*. Notwithstanding of which accounts and how many are impacted by a given transaction, the fundamental accounting equation of assets equals liabilities plus capital will always hold.

Triple-entry accounting (TEA) is described as an enhancement to conventional DEA where the accounting entries are cryptographically sealed by a third entity (the blockchain). Blockchain technology may represent the next step for accounting: instead of keeping separate records based on transaction receipts, companies can write their transactions directly into a joint register, creating an interlocking system of enduring accounting records. As all entries are distributed and cryptographically sealed, falsifying or destroying them to conceal activity is practically impossible (Dai and Vasarhelyi 2017).

The companies would benefit in numerous ways: standardization would allow auditors to verify a large portion of the most important data supporting the financial statements automatically (Appelbaum and Nehmer 2017). The efforts, time and, hence, costs necessary to conduct an audit would decline considerably. Auditors could spend freed up time on areas they can add more value, for example, on very complex transactions or on internal control mechanisms.

## Decentralized Finance

Decentralized finance (DeFi) can be understood as an open financial ecosystem (Birrer et al. 2023). Operating without the need for a trusted third party, DeFi aims to give users an alternative to the traditional financial world. For instance, when a decentralized P2P network is fully operational, everybody can participate in the network to carry out traditional economic transactions like payment, investing, lending, and borrowing. These instances remove the reliance on intermediaries to facilitate the flow of transactions. Besides, no central entity can monopolize the network and exclude others from participating as is the case in the current financial system. Due to its high level of accessibility, DeFi is arguably well suited for emerging economies and population groups with limited access to traditional financial services.

# Identity

Any service in the cloud is exposed to trust, security, and privacy threats that can compromise the identity of end users. Advanced identity management systems (IMS) in addition to providing improved end-user experience also offer novel identity-related features (Royer 2013). These systems are designed to deal with authentication and authorization processes, enabling single sign-on and methods to exchange end-user information between different entities and/or domains. End-users are granted secure access to different resources or services using a single identity by establishing trust links among different providers while preserving end users privacy.

IMS are exposed to a number of threats that can compromise its behavior when malicious users or entities try to subvert the system. The primary types of threats are:

a. Trust Threats: Service and identity providers require an infrastructure where all the involved parties must be trusted for specific purposes depending on their role. If one of the parties acts maliciously, then the rest of the participants could be exposed to different risks. IMS need to deploy mechanisms to allow entities to trust each other, although in some scenarios, the trust mechanisms may themselves introduce their own threat vulnerabilities unless those have also been taken into account.

b. Security Threats: IMS managing identity-related information are vulnerable to attacks due to the fact that they potentially manage sensitive information. IMS need to avoid any threat that allows an attacker to affect the system negatively or steal information of the end users or steal the identity of the end user itself or to interfere in the communication or interrupt services.

c. Privacy Threats: End users usually want to keep the information of their digital identities secret. Many organizations do not need the real identities of their end users, but they certainly want to record their behavior in terms of services accessed and used respectively. IMS have to deploy mechanisms to preserve end users' privacy, including:

  i. Anonymity, where a service provider cannot know the real identity of an end-user
  ii. Unlikability, where a service provider cannot link different end-user's accesses
  iii. Untraceability, where an identity provider cannot know the services accessed by the end-users

The Aadhaar project undertaken by the Unique Identification Authority of India (UIDAI) had the mission of identifying 1.2 billion citizens of India uniquely and reliably to build the largest biometric identity repository in the world (while eliminating duplication and fake identities) and provide an online, anytime anywhere, multifactor authentication service. This made possible to identify any individual and get it authenticated at any time, from any place in India, in less than a second. One of the most significant use of Aadhaar is that it allows the user to get all government benefits. When they connect it to their bank, all payments are sent immediately to the beneficiary's bank account. As a result, service providers can concentrate on their products and services rather than worrying about verification and other systemic issues.

A snapshot of Aadhaar digital identity system has the following components:

1. Identification: A biometric system.
2. Authentication: A digital online evidence of identity and address. Because the biometric information is available online, authorized entities can cross-verify and confirm the identity before proceeding with the process of providing services and subsidies.
3. Authorization: The process of ascertaining whether a particular service or subsidy can be given to this person.

## Trust

The Internet offers individuals the ability to obscure or conceal their identities. The resulting anonymity reduces the cues normally used in judgments of trust. The identity is critical for developing trust relations; it allows us to base our trust on the past history of interactions with an entity. Anonymity causes mistrust because identity is associated with accountability, and in the absence of identity, accountability cannot be enforced. The opacity extends immediately from identity to personal characteristics. It is impossible to infer whether the entity or individual we transact with is who it pretends to be, as the transactions occur between entities separated in time and distance. Finally, there are no guarantees that the entities we transact with fully understand the role they have assumed (Paliszkiewicz and Chen 2022).

There are primarily two ways of determining trust:

- Policies reveal the conditions to obtain trust and the actions to take when some of the conditions are met. Policies require the verification of credentials.
- Reputation is a quality attributed to an entity based on a relatively long history of interactions with or possibly observations of the entity.

Recommendations are based on trust decisions made by others and filtered through the perspective of the entity assessing the trust.

# Privacy

Digital privacy is of growing importance with the increasing amount of personal digital information transmitted, utilized, and stored in various public, private, and nonprofit organizations. The increasing adoption and use of e-government information and transactions have accelerated the collection of personal information in a digital format. Sensitive income and other personal finance information are also included in the transactions. The increasing linkage and sharing of information from various organizations and agencies to provide customer-centric services is likely to lead to concerns about digital privacy if there are no additional safeguards for potential profiling as the result of such linkages. Similarly, such exposures and the possibilities for combining the information to create personal profiles for sales or marketing purposes constitute an invasion into our digital privacy. An added complication is the growing power of Internet search engines and applications that even allow an information consolidation company to integrate all public records online to create personal profiles for many individuals and then to sell them for profit.

Edward Snowden's disclosures of top-secret NSA documents in 2013 were crucial in exposing how vulnerable people are to privacy invasions and marked an inflection point in how we protect sensitive information. Among other things, Snowden showed how in the name of national security the NSA ordinarily collected phone records of millions of citizens and how the NSA conducts mass surveillance activities globally and spies on hundreds of world leaders. The metadata collected were not used for the purpose originally intended, and thus, these operations violated many federal laws. Moreover, most of these data sources were from mobile communications and social media companies that promise to protect our privacy but actually give the NSA access to our data. On top of this, Snowden exposed the casual approach to security that many companies were taking (e.g., by not using SSL encryption) and which routinely exposed user account data.

A growing array of information and communication technologies are posing increasingly serious threats to digital privacy:

  i. Big data gathered from social media, sensors, and mobile devices, or even for academic and research purposes, could have serious privacy implications.

    ii. Facebook that stores personal/group pictures and information; location-based technologies that can track our movements via phones, and so on.

   iii. Google Maps that can show satellite images of an individual's property surveillance cameras that can collect video footage of individuals' activities

The challenge is to strike a dynamic balance between privacy and access in the digital era. The overarching goal is to find ways to maximize both privacy and access, that is, to find an alternative that protects individuals' privacy while simultaneously improving access to information. Such a balance in protecting digital privacy would a moving target depending on the capability of current technologies intruding into personal digital privacy. There will be an increasing need for a more coordinated approach between the protection of digital privacy and assurance of digital security because the main source of the loss of digital privacy may be a security breach of an information system with customers' personal information (Adams 2021).

## Security

The goal of security is to protect an organization's information assets and infrastructure from accidental or malicious disclosure, modification, misuse, and erasure (Shukla 2020). Whereas people—especially the trusted people inside the organization—are the most important factor in information integrity and protection, the technology of security also plays a vital role. Technical controls protect information assets and infrastructure primarily from people outside the organization—those who are not trusted. Security technology plays an important role for insiders, too, through access controls and audit capabilities. These help to reinforce accountability and also provide valuable information during investigations.

  1. Confidentiality: The operation of an organization necessitates the concealment of some information from others. It ensures that confidential information can be accessed only by an authorized person and should be reserved away from all those who are not authorized to

access them. Confidentiality is a concept that may be implemented at many levels of a process. Confidentiality can be compromised by the loss of a laptop containing data, a person looking over our shoulder while we type a password, an e-mail attachment being sent to the wrong person, an attacker penetrating our systems, or similar issues.

As an example, if we consider the case of a person withdrawing money from an ATM:

- The user will likely seek to maintain the confidentiality of the personal identification number (PIN) that allows him/her, in combination with his/her ATM card, to draw funds from the ATM.
- The owner of the ATM will hopefully maintain the confidentiality of the account number, balance, and any other information needed to communicate to the bank from which the funds are being drawn.
- The bank will maintain the confidentiality of the transaction with the ATM and the balance change in the account after the funds have been withdrawn.

If at any point in the transaction confidentiality is compromised, the results could be bad for the user, the owner of the ATM, and the bank, potentially resulting in what is known in the information security field as a breach.

2. Integrity: Integrity refers to the ability to prevent our data from being changed in an unauthorized or undesirable manner. This could mean the unauthorized change or deletion of our data or portions of our data, or it could mean an authorized, but undesirable, change or deletion of our data.

It is not enough to limit access at the system level in order to maintain integrity but also necessary to ensure that system users can only change information that they have been legally permitted to change. To maintain integrity, we not only need to have the means to prevent unauthorized changes to our data but also need the ability to reverse authorized changes that need to be undone.

Integrity violations are not always the consequence of malevolent behavior; a system disruption, such as a power surge, can also cause undesirable changes in data.

3. Availability: Availability refers to the ability to access our data when we need it. Loss of availability can refer to a wide variety of breaks anywhere in the chain that allows us access to our data. Such issues can also result from power loss, operating system or application problems, network attacks, compromise of a system, hardware failures, unplanned software downtime, and network bandwidth challenges—which are all examples of nonmalicious threats to availability.

When such issues are caused by an outside party, such as an attacker, they are commonly referred to as a denial of service (DoS) attack. A DoS attack occurs when a hacker floods a server with unnecessary requests, overloading it and reducing service for legitimate users.

The various types of attacks corresponding to these aspects of security are:

i. Interception: Interception attacks allow unauthorized users to access our data, applications, or environments and are primarily an attack against confidentiality. Interception might take the form of unauthorized file viewing or copying, eavesdropping on phone conversations, or reading e-mail, and can be conducted against data.

ii. Modification: Modification attacks involve tampering with our asset. Such attacks might primarily be considered an integrity attack but could also represent an availability attack. If we access a file in an unauthorized manner and alter the data it contains, we have affected the integrity of the data contained in the file. However, if we consider the case where the file in question is a configuration file that manages how a particular service behaves, perhaps one that is acting as a web server, we might affect the availability of that service by changing the contents of the file.

iii. Interruption: Interruption attacks cause our assets to become unusable or unavailable for our use, on a temporary or permanent basis. Interruption attacks often affect availability but can be an attack on integrity as well. In the case of a DoS attack on a mail server, we would classify this as an availability attack. In the case of an attacker manipulating the processes on which a database runs in order to prevent access to the data it contains, we might consider this an integrity attack, due to the possible loss or corruption of data, or we might consider it a combination of the two. We might also consider such a database attack to be a modification attack rather than an interruption attack.

iv. Fabrication: Fabrication attacks involve generating data, processes, communications, or other similar activities with a system. Fabrication attacks primarily affect integrity but could be considered an availability attack as well. If we generate spurious information in a database, this would be considered to be a fabrication attack. In the sense of an availability attack, if we generate enough additional processes, network traffic, e-mail, web traffic, or nearly anything else that consumes resources, we can potentially render the service that handles such traffic unavailable to legitimate users of the system.

### IoT Security Framework

Details are available in the Appendix section (**A.12.1 IoT Security Framework**) available online.

# Blockchain Technology

Blockchain technology can be seen as a disruptive and revolutionary technology that can be compared with the revolution sparked by the WWW and the Internet in general. As the Internet can be seen as a means for sharing information, so blockchain technologies can be seen as a way sharing value. The consensus mechanism allows agents to transfer *value* without having a third party involved in the process, which guarantees that the source actually owns that value which it wants to transfer and which guarantees that the recipient receives the value being transferred. The elimination of this third trusted party is a major breakthrough (Tanwar 2022).

The disruptive potential of the consensus algorithm is enormous. The whole transaction history (from the first that occurred) is accessible by anyone (any agent that wants to check what happened from the genesis), and it cannot be changed. The fact that all the transactions are public and it is not possible to delete them is the key which lets the consensus algorithm work. Consensus is linked with another two elements necessary to let this technology work: P2P networks and cryptography. The blockchain is built upon a P2P network, and anyone willing to join the network can do it without asking permission from anyone. Each node of the network exposes a constantly updated version of the blockchain, and this fact gives the possibility (to each node) to verify old and new transactions and to decide if they are valid or not.

The idea of a smart contract was originally described by cryptographer Nick Szabo in 1997. Smart contracts are self-enforcing agreements, that is, contracts, implemented through a computer program whose execution enforces the terms of the contract. The blockchain technology is the instrument for delivering the trust model envisaged by smart contracts as a kind of digital vending machine. Smart contracts are particular decentralized applications that can be seen as computer programs executed by participants in a blockchain, which is used as a backbone infrastructure for running it. As smart contracts are stored on a blockchain, they are public and transparent, immutable, and decentralized. Immutability means that when a smart contract is created, it cannot be changed again. The idea is to get rid of a central control authority, entity, or organization that both parties must trust and delegate such a role to the correct execution of a computer program.

Blockchain technology uses a decentralized and disseminated database and is composed of a sequence of blocks. These blocks consist of a list of transactions that have taken place, and also a hash key of previous block along with a timestamp. Thus, it is a linked list concept, meaning the blocks are interlinked in chronological sequence. It creates complete history commencing with the first block to the latest generated block.

> Hash key is a one-way function that is used to interlink the blocks. A hash key is made through a hash function that represents a mathematical algorithm that transforms any input (numbers, alphabets, media files) of any length into a fixed sized output.

The hash function plays a significant role to detect any modifications within the block. These blocks are updated on a continuous basis, replicated, and circulated to each node present in the network and also maintain integrity and timestamps of the data. As soon as the data inside the block is changed, the hash of the block also gets changed.

Additional details are available in the Appendix section (**A.12.2 Blockchain Technology**) available online.

# Conclusion

The chapter started with a description of aspects and issues of governance, identity, trust, privacy, and security in the operating environment of a startup. As an illustration, it describes a seven-layer security framework for an IoT application. It then introduced blockchain technology as the panacea for addressing all these constellation of requirements. Blockchain technology uses a decentralized and disseminated database and is composed of a sequence of blocks. These blocks consist of a list of transactions that have taken place, and also a hash key of previous block along with a timestamp. People involved in any service can only add records to it, not change it. Blockchain is a linked list concept, meaning the blocks are interlinked in chronological sequence—it creates a complete history commencing with the first block to the latest generated block.

In a permissionless network, everyone is equal, yet this opens the door to system abuse. Therefore, an appropriate consensus mechanism is necessary to make common judgments about the expansion of the underlying blockchain system and avoid network behavior that is detrimental to the system's overall health. The immutability of blockchain technology is a perfect property for preventing censorship of any type. The immutability of a blockchain is ensured via cryptographic hashing, a consensus process, and decentralization. After giving an overview of the features and characteristics of the blockchain technology, the chapter ended by explaining how the incorporation of blockchain into the supply chain system resulted in an automated, efficient, trusted and secure SCM system.

*This chapter described the critical issues of governance, identity, trust, privacy, and security. It then introduced blockchain as the panacea for addressing all these constellation of requirements. It highlighted how the decentralized aspects of blockchain can give rise to unique solutions like TEA and DeFi.*

# References

Adams, C. 2021. *Introduction to Privacy Enhancing Technologies: A Classification-Based Approach to Understanding PETs*. Cham: Springer.

Agarwal, C.C. 2018. *Neural Networks and Deep Learning-A Textbook*. Cham: Springer.

Agarwal, S. and S. Mishra. 2021. *Responsible AI: Implementing Ethical and Unbiased Algorithms*. Cham: Springer.

Akaev, A.A., A.I. Rudskoy, and T. Deveza. 2021. "Technological Substitution of Jobs in the Digital Economy and Shift in Labor Demand Towards Advanced Qualifications." In *The Economics of Digital Transformation: Approaching Non-stable and Uncertain Digitalized Production Systems*, eds. T. Devezas, J. Leitão, and A. Sarygulov. Cham: Springer.

Albert, M.V., L. Lin, M.J. Spector, and L.S. Dunn, eds. 2022. *Bridging Human Intelligence and Artificial Intelligence*. Cham: Springer.

Altshuller, G.S. 1984. *Creativity as an Exact Science: The Theory of the Solution of the Inventive Problems*. Gordon and Breach Science Publishers.

Androutsellis-Theotokis, S., D. Spinellis, M. Kechagia, and G. Gousios. 2010. "Open Source Software: A Survey From 10,000 Feet." *Foundations and Trends® in Technology, Information and Operations Management* 4, pp. 187–347.

Ang, Y.Q., A. Chia, and S. Saghafian. 2022. "Using Machine Learning to Demystify Startups' Funding, Post-Money Valuation, and Success." In *Innovative Technology at the Interface of Finance and Operations Volume I*, eds. V. Babich, J.R. Birge, and G. Hillary. Cham: Springer.

Annarelli, A., C. Battistella, and F. Nonino. 2019. *The Road to Servitization: How Product Service Systems Can Disrupt Companies' Business Models*. Cham: Springer.

Ante, S.E. 2008. *Creative Capital: Georges Doriot and the Birth of Venture Capital*. Boston: Harvard Business Press.

Appelbaum, D. and R. Nehmer. 2017. *Designing and Auditing Accounting Systems Based on Blockchain and Distributed Ledger Principles*. Upper Montclair, NJ: Feliciano School of Business.

Argote, L. 2013. *Organizational Learning-Creating, Retaining and Transferring Knowledge*. 2nd ed. New York, NY: Springer.

Attfield, R. 2021. *Environmental Thought: A Short History*. Medford: Polity Press.

Banasiewicz, A. 2021. *Organizational Learning in the Age of Data*. Cham: Springer.

Barker, R. 2016. *Bioscience: Lost in Translation How Precision Medicine Closes the Innovation Gap*. Oxford: Oxford University Press.

Belleflamme, P. and M. Peitz. 2021. *The Economics of Platforms: Concepts and Strategy*. Cambridge: Cambridge University Press.

Belleghem, S.V. 2015. *When Digital Becomes Human: The Transformation of Customer Relationships*. London: Kogan Page.

Bessen, J. 2022. *The New Goliaths: How Corporations Use Software to Dominate Industries, Kill Innovation and Undermine Regulation*. New Haven: Yale University Press.

Bhimani, A. 2022. *Financial Management for Technology Startups: A Handbook for Growth*. 2nd ed. London: Kogan Page.

Birrer, T.K., D. Amstutz, and P. Wenger. 2023. *Decentralized Finance: From Core Concepts to DeFi Protocols for Financial Transactions*. Cham: Springer.

Bishwash, S.K. and S.K. Addya. 2021. *Cloud Network Management: An IoT Based Framework*. Boca Raton: CRC Press.

Bjorner, D. 2021. *Domain Science and Engineering-A Foundation for Software Development*. Cham: Springer.

Bonomi, A. 2020. *Technology Dynamic: The Generation of Innovative Ideas and Their Transformation Into New Technologies*. Boca Raton: CRC Press.

Bredin, K. and J. Soderlund. 2011. *Human Resource Management in Project-Based Organizations: The HR Quadriad Framework*. New York, NY: Palgrave Macmillan.

Brézillon, P. and A.J. Gonzalez, eds. 2014. *Context in Computing: A Cross-Disciplinary Approach for Modeling the Real World*. New York, NY: Springer.

Brinkmann, R. 2016. *Introduction to Sustainability*. Hoboken: Wiley-Blackwell.

Brown, B.R. 2023. *Engineering Intelligent Systems: System Engineering and Design With Artificial Intelligence, Visual Modeling, and System Thinking*. Hoboken: Wiley.

Burnett, K. 1998. *The Project Management Paradigm*. London: Springer-Verlag.

Byrant, J.A., M.A. Atherton, and M.W. Collins. 2007. *Design and Information in Biology: From Molecules to Systems*. Southampton: WIT Press

Callahan K.R., G.S. Stetz and L.M. Brooks. 2011. *Project Management Accounting: Budgeting, Tracking, and Reporting Costs and Profitability*. Hoboken: Wiley.

Calvo, G. 2020. *Journey of the Future Enterprise: How to Compete in the Age of Moonshot Leadership and Exponential Organizations*. Barcelona: Libros de Cabecera

Cantamessa, M. and F. Montagna, 2023. *Management of Innovation and Product Development, 2nd Ed-Integrating Business and Technology Perspectives*. London: Springer-Verlag.

Cao, L. 2015. *Metasynthetic Computing and Engineering of Complex Systems*. London: Springer-Verlag.

Carreira, P., V. Amaral, and H. Vangheluwe, eds. 2020. *Foundations of Multi-Paradigm Modelling for Cyber-Physical Systems*. Cham: Springer.

Carter, R.J. 2021. *Cognitive Advantage: How Artificial Intelligence Is Changing the Rules for Winning in Business and Government*. Mayhill Publishing.

Caruso, G.R. 2020. *The Art of Business Valuation: Accurately Valuing a New Business*. Hoboken: Wiley.

Chandra, S. 2018. *Aesthetics: Quantification and Deconstruction a Case Study in Motorcycles*. Singapore: Springer.

Chechurin, L., ed. 2016. *Research and Practice on the Theory of Inventive Problem Solving (TRIZ): Linking Creativity, Engineering and Innovation*. Cham: Springer.

Chowdhury, R. 2019. *Systems Thinking for Management Consultants: Introducing Holistic Flexibility*. Singapore: Springer.

Christensen, C.M. 2000. *The Innovators Dilemma: When Technologies Cause Great Firms to Fail*. Boston: Harvard Business Review Press.

Clatworthy, S.D. 2019. *The Experience-Centric Organisation: How to Win Through Customer Experience*. Sebastopol: O'Reilly Media.

Cohen, J.A. 2005. *Invisible Assets: Valuation and Economic Benefit*. Hoboken: Wiley.

Craig, A.B. 2013. *Understanding Augmented Reality: Concepts and Applications*. Waltham: Elsevier.

Cunningham, W. 1992. *The WyCash Portfolio Management System*. Experience Report, OOPSLA'92.

Daft, R.L. 2020. *Organization Theory and Design*. 13th ed. London: Thompson.

Dai, J. and M.A. Vasarhelyi. 2017. "Toward Blockchain-Based Accounting and Assurance." *Journal of Information Systems* 31, no. 3, pp. 5–21.

David, D., S. Gopalan, and S. Ramachandran. 2021. "The Startup Environment and Funding Activity in India." In *Investment in Startups and Small Business Financing*, eds. F. Taghizadeh-Hesary, N. Yoshino, C.J. Kim, P.J. Morgan, and D. Yoon. London: World Scientific.

Davis, S. 1987. *Future Perfect*. New York, NY: Basic Books.

Dewey, J. 1929. *The Quest for Certainty* Minton. Balch and Company.

Dewey, J. 1934. *Art as Experience*. Minton and Company.

Dewey, J. 1938. *Education and Experience*. New York, NY: Simon and Schuster.

Dohn, N.B., ed. 2018. *Designing for Learning in a Networked World*. New York, NY: Routledge

Du, K.L. and M.N.S. Swamy. 2014. *Neural Networks and Statistical Learning*. 2nd ed. London: Springer.

Duffey, C. 2019. *Superhuman Innovation: Transforming Business With Artificial Intelligence*. London: Kogan Page.

Durcan, J. 2016. *Outsourcing and the Virtual Organization: The Incredible Shrinking Company*. Cornerstone Digital

ED: World Commission on Environment and Development. 1987. *Our Common Future*. Oxford: Oxford University Press.

Edmonds, S.C. 2014. *The Culture Engine: A Framework for Driving Results, Inspiring Your Employees, and Transforming Your Workplace*. Hoboken: Wiley.

El Emary, I.M.M., A. Brzozowska, and D. Bubel. 2020. *Management of Organizational Culture as a Stabilizer of Changes: Organizational Culture Management Dilemmas*. Boca Raton: CRC Press.

Ellis, G. 2016. *Project Management in Product Development: Leadership Skills and Management Techniques to Deliver Great Products*. Waltham: Elsevier.

Espindola, D. and M.W. Wright. 2021. *The Exponential Era: Strategies to Stay Ahead of the Curve in an Era of Chaotic Changes and Disruptive Forces*. Hoboken: Wiley

European Commission. 2014. *The 2014 EU Industrial R&D Investment Scoreboard*. European Commission—Joint Research Centre.

European Commission. 2015. *The 2015 EU Industrial R&D Investment Scoreboard*. European Commission—Joint Research Centre.

Fahmy, H.M.A. 2016. *Wireless Sensor Networks: Concepts, Applications, Experimentation and Analysis*. Singapore: Springer.

Felderer, M. and G.H. Travasos. 2020. *Contemporary Empirical Methods in Software Engineering*. Cham: Springer.

Feldman, D.N. 2013. *The Entrepreneur's Growth Startup Handbook: 7 Secrets to Venture Funding and Successful Growth*. Hoboken: Wiley.

Furrer, F.J. 2019. *Future-Proof Software-Systems-A Sustainable Evolution Strategy*. Wiesbaden: Springer-Verlag.

Galbriath, J.R. 2014. *Designing Organizations: Strategy, Structure, and Process at the Business Unit and Enterprise Levels*. San Francisco: Jossey-Bass

Galitsky, B. 2019. *Developing Enterprise Chatbots: Learning Linguistic Structures*. Cham: Springer.

Ganguli, R., S. Adhikari, S. Chakraborty, and M. Ganguli. 2023. *Digital Twin: A Dynamic System and Computing Perspective*. Boca Raton: CRC Press.

Gassmann, O., A. Schuhmacher, M.V. Zedtwitz, and G. Reepmeyer. 2018. *Leading Pharmaceutical Innovation: How to Win the Life Science Race*. 3rd ed. Cham: Springer.

Gebauer, J. and D. Lowman. 2008. *Closing the Engagement Gap: How Great Companies Unlock Employee Potential for Superior Results*. Portfolio.

Ghaboussi, J. 2018. *Soft Computing in Engineering*. Boca Raton: CRC Press.

Gilmore, J.H. and J. Pine. 2000. *Markets of One: Creating Customer-Unique Value Through Mass Customization*. Boston: Harvard Business School Publishing.

Goldin, D., S.A. Smolka, and P. Wegner, eds. 2006. *Interactive Computation: The New Paradigm*. Berlin: Springer-Verlag.

Gratacap, A., S.B. Letaifa, and T. Isckia. 2018. *Understanding Business Ecosystems: How Firms Succeed in the New World of Convergence*. De Boeck Supérieur.

Green, J.S. and S. Daniels. 2020. *Digital Governance: Leading and Thriving in a World of Fast-Changing Technologies*. Boca Raton: CRC Press.

Guillen, M. 2021. *The Platform Paradox: How Digital Businesses Succeed in an Ever-Changing Global Marketplace*. Philadelphia: Wharton School Press

Halt, G.B., J.C. Donch, A.R. Stiles, and R. Fesnak, 2017. *Intellectual Property and Financial Strategies for Technology Startups*. Cham: Springer.

Hilbush, G. 2021. *In Silico Dreams: How Artificial Intelligence and Biotech Will Create the Medicines of the Future*. Hoboken: Wiley.

Hilken, T., D.I. Keeling, K. de Ruyter, D. Mahr, and M. Chylinski. 2020. "Seeing Eye to Eye: Social Augmented Reality and Shared Decision Making in the Marketplace." *Journal of the Academy of Marketing Science* 48, pp. 143–164.

Hisrich, R.D. and V. Ramadani. 2017. *Effective Entrepreneurial Management: Strategy, Planning, Risk Management, and Organization*. Cham: Springer.

Hopgood, A.A. 2022. *Intelligent Systems for Engineers and Scientists: A Practical Guide to Artificial Intelligence*. 4th ed. Boca Raton: CRC Press.

Huang, X., G. Jin, and W. Ruan. 2023. *Machine Learning Safety*. Cham: Springer.

Ismail, S. 2014. *Why New Organizations Are Ten times Better, Faster, and Cheaper Than Yours (and What to Do About It)*. New York, NY: Diversion Publications.

Johannesson, P. and E. Perjons. 2021. *An Introduction to Design Science*. 2nd ed. Cham: Springer.

Johnson, B., W.W. Woolfolk, R. Miller, and C. Johnson. 2005. *Flexible Software Design-Systems: Systems Development for Changing Requirements*. Boca Raton: Auerbach Publications.

Kagermann, H., W. Wahlster, and J. Helbig. 2013. *Securing the Future of German Manufacturing Industry. Recommendations for Implementing the Strategic Initiative INDUSTRIE 4.0*. Technical report, National Academy of Science and Engineering (ACATECH).

Kahneman, D. and A. Tversky. 2000. *Choices, Values, and Frames*. Cambridge University Press.

Kahraman, C. and S. Cebi. 2020. *Customer Oriented Product Design: Intelligent and Fuzzy Techniques*. Cham: Springer.

Kale, V. 2014. *Inverting the Paradox of Excellence: How Companies Use Variations for Business Excellence and How Enterprise Variations Are Enabled by SAP*. Boca Raton: CRC Press.

Kale, V. 2016. *Enhancing Enterprise Intelligence: Leveraging ERP, CRM, SCM, PLM, BPM, and BI*. Boca Raton: CRC Press.

Kale, V. 2017. *Agile Network Businesses: Collaboration, Coordination, and Competitive Advantage*. Boca Raton: CRC Press.

Kale, V. 2019. *Digital Transformation of Enterprise Architecture*. Boca Raton: CRC Press.

Kale, V. 2020. *Parallel Computing Architectures and APIs: IoT Big Data Stream Processing*. Boca Raton: CRC Press.

Kaliraj, P. and T. Devi. 2022. *Artificial Intelligence: Theory, Models and Applications*. Boca Raton: CRC Press.

Kamath, M. and J. Liu. 2021. *Explainable Artificial Intelligence: An Introduction to Interpretable Machine Learning*. Cham: Springer.

Kamath, U., K.L. Graham, and W. Rmara. 2022. *Transformers for Machine Learning: A Deep Dive*. Boca Raton: CRC Press.

Kaneko, T. and N. Yoshioka. 2022. "Methods for Ensuring the Overall Safety of Machine Learning Systems." In *Handbook on Artificial Intelligence-Empowered Applied Software Engineering*, eds. M. Virvou, G.A. Tsihrintzis, N.G. Bourbakis, and L.C. Jain, vol. 1. Cham: Springer.

Kansal, P., D. Sharma, and M. Kumar. 2020. "Introduction to Fog Data Analytics for IoT Applications." In *Fog Data Analytics for IoT Applications: Next Generation Process Model With State of the Art Technologies*, eds. S. Tanwar. Singapore: Springer.

Kaschny, M. and M. Nolden. 2018. *Innovation and Transformation: Basics, Implementation and Optimization*. Cham: Springer.

Kates, A. and J.R. Galbriath, 2007. *Designing Your Organization Using the Star Model to Solve 5 Critical Design Challenges*. San Francisco: Jossey-Bass.

Keathley, J.D. and H.J. Harrington. 2020. *Structuring Your Organization for Innovation*. ASQ Quality Press.

Kelly, R. 2019. *Constructing Leadership 4.0: Swarm Leadership and the Fourth Industrial Revolution*. Cham: Palgrave Macmillan.

Kerzner, H. 2017. *Project Management: A Systems Approach to Planning, Scheduling and Controlling*. 12th ed. Hoboken: Wiley.

Kim, J., T. Davis, and L. Hong. 2022. "Augmented Intelligence: Enhancing Human Decision Making." In *Bridging Human Intelligence and Artificial Intelligence*, eds. M.V. Albert, L. Lin, M.J. Spector, and L.S. Dunn. Cham: Springer.

Kraner, J. 2018. *Innovation in High Reliability Ambidextrous Organizations: Analytical Solutions Toward Increasing Innovative Activity*. Cham: Springer.

Kuratko, D.F. and J.S. Hornsby. 2018. *New Venture Management: The Entrepreneur's Roadmap*. 2nd ed. New York, NY: Routledge.

Kuratko, D.F., M.G. Goldsby, J.S. Hornsby. 2019. *Corporate Innovation: Disruptive Thinking in Organizations*. New York, NY: Routledge.

Lambrechts, W., S. Sinha, J. Abdallah, and J. Prinsloo. 2019. *Extending Moore's Law Through Advanced Semiconductor Design and Processing Techniques*. Boca Raton: CRC Press.

Lank, E. 2006. *Collaborative Advantage: How Organizations Win by Working Together*. New York, NY: Palgrave Macmillan.

Lee, R.Y. 2013. *Software Engineering: A Hands-On Approach*. Atlantis Press.

Liou, F.W. 2008. *Rapid Prototyping and Engineering Applications: Toolbox for Prototype Development*. Boca Raton: CRC Press.

Loshin, D. and A. Reifer. 2013. *Using Information to Develop a Culture of Customer Centricity: Customer Centricity, Analytics and Information Utilization*. Waltham: Elsevier.

Luca, M. and M.H. Bazerman. 2020. *The Power of Experiments: Decision Making in a Data-Driven World*. Cambridge: The MIT Press.

Ma, S. and J.M. Spector. 2022. Human Intelligence and Artificial Intelligence: Divergent or Complementary Intelligences? In *Bridging Human Intelligence and Artificial Intelligence*, eds. M.V. Albert, L. Lin, M.J. Spector, and L.S. Dunn. Cham: Springer.

Machado, C. and J.P. Davim, eds. 2014. *Human Resource Management and Technical Challenges*. Cham: Springer.

Machado, C. and J.P. Davim, eds. 2019. *Management Science: Foundations and Innovations*. Cham: Springer.

Malecki, E.J. and B. Moriset. 2008. *The Digital Organization, Production Processes and Regional Developments*. New York, NY: Routledge.

Marcham, A. 2021. *Understanding Infrastructure Edge Computing: Concepts, Technologies and Considerations: Concepts, Technologies and Considerations*. Hoboken: Wiley

Mariotti, J.L. 2008. *The Complexity Crisis: Why Too Many Products, Markets and Customers Are Crippling Your Company—And What to Do About It*. Avon: Platinum Press.

Marti, M. 2007. *Complexity Management: Optimizing Product Architecture of Industrial Products*. Gabler.

Maslow, A. 1943. "A Theory of Human Motivation." *Psychological Review* 50, no. 4, pp. 370–396.

McAteer, P. 2019. *Sustainability Is the New Advantage: Leadership, Change and the Future of Business*. London: Anthem Press.

McTear, M. 2021. *Conversational AI: Dialogue Systems, Conversational Agents, and Chatbots*. Morgan & Claypool Publishers.

Metrick, A. and A. Yasuda. 2011. *Venture Capital & the Finance of Innovation*. 2nd ed. Hoboken: Wiley.

Mihelj, M., D. Novak, and S. Begus. 2014. *Virtual Reality Technology and Applications*. Dordrecht: Springer.

Mintzberg, H. 1979. *The Structuring of Organizations*.

Mishra, C.S. 2015. *Getting Funded: Proof-of-Concept, Due Diligence, Risk and Reward*. New York, NY: Palgrave Macmillan.

Misra, S., C. Roy, and A. Mukherjee. 2021. *Introduction to Industrial Internet of Things and Industry 4.0*. Boca Raton: CRC Press.

Modrâak, V. 2017. *Mass Customized Manufacturing: Theoretical Concepts and Practical Approaches*. Boca Raton: CRC Press.

Morcol, G. 2023. *Complex Governance Networks: Foundational Concepts and Practical Implications*. New York, NY: Boca Raton: CRC Press.

Moretti, A. 2017. *The Network Organization: A Governance Perspective on Structure, Dynamics and Performance*. Cham: Palgrave Macmillan.

Moro-Visconti, R. 2022. *The Valuation of Digital Intangibles: Technology, Marketing, and the Metaverse*. 2nd ed. Cham: Palgrave Macmillan.

Mukherjee, P.K. 2022. *Decision-Making: Concepts, Methods, Techniques.* New Delhi: Sage Publications.

Nandi, A. and A.K. Pal. 2022. *Interpreting Machine Learning Models: Learn Model Interpretability and Explainability Methods.* Delaware: Apress.

Newbery, P. and K. Farnham. 2013. *Experience Design: A Framework for Integrating Brand, Experience, and Value.* Hoboken: Wiley.

Open Source Initiative: Licenses & Standards. n.d. https://opensource.org/licenses.

Osburg, T. and C. Lohrmann. 2017. *Sustainability in a Digital World: New Opportunities Through New Technologies.* Cham: Springer.

Pal, S. and N. Tripathi. 2022. "Digital Market Scenario in India: A Case Study on "Unicorn" Indian Digital Start-Ups." In *Industry 4.0 in Small and Medium-Sized Enterprises (SMEs): Opportunities, Challenges, and Solutions,* eds. K. Kotecha, S. Kumar, A. Bongale, and R. Suresh. Boca Raton: CRC Press.

Pal, S., V.G. Díaz, and D.N. Le, eds. 2020. *IoT: Security and Privacy Paradigm.* Boca Raton: CRC Press.

Paliszkiewicz, J. and K. Chen. 2022. *Trust, Organizations and the Digital Economy: Theory and Practice.* New York, NY: Routledge.

Pandeeswari, S.T., S. Padmavathi, and N. Hemamalini. 2020. Engineering Full Stack IoT Systems With Distributed Processing Architecture—Software Engineering Challenges, Architectures and Tools. In *Journey Towards Bio-inspired Techniques in Software Engineering,* eds. J. Singh, S. Bilgaiyan, B.S.P. Mishra, and S. Dehuri. Cham: Springer.

Passiante, G., ed. 2020. *Innovative Entrepreneurship in Action: From High-Tech to Digital Entrepreneurship.* Cham: Springer.

Paul, S.M., D.S. Mytelka, C.T. Dunwiddie, C.C. Persinger, B.H. Munos, S.R. Lindborg, and A.L. Schacht. 2010. "How to improve R&D Productivity: The Pharmaceutical Industry's Grand Challenge." *Nature Reviews Drug Discovery* 9, pp. 203–214.

Perens, B. and M. Sroka. 2007. *The Open Source Definition.*

Peters, T.J. and R.H. Waterman. 1980. *In Search of Excellence: Lessons From America's Best-Run Companies.* New York, NY: Oxford University Press.

Petrov, V. 2023. *Talented Thinking: TRIZ.* Cham: Springer.

Pine, J. and J.H. Gilmore. 2011. *The Experience Economy.* Boston: Harvard Business School Publishing.

Pine, J. and S. Davis. 1993 *Mass customization: The New Frontier in Business Competition.* Boston: Harvard Business Press.

Pinto, J.F. 2016. *Project Management: Achieving Competitive Advantage.* Pearson.

Poltorak, A.I. and P.J. Lerner. 2011. *Essentials of Intellectual Property-Law, Economics, and Strategy.* 2nd ed. Hoboken, New Jersey.

Poole, D.L. and A.K. Macworth. 2017. *Artificial Intelligence: Foundations of Computational Agents.* 2nd ed. Cambridge: Cambridge University Press.

Primrose, S.B. 2020. *Biomimetics: Nature Inspired Design and Innovation.* Hoboken: Wiley.

Priyadarshini, R., R.M. Mehra, A. Sehgal, and P.J. Singh. 2023. *Artificial Intelligence: Applications and Innovations.* Boca Raton: CRC Press.

Project Management Institute. 2021. *A Guide to the Project Management Body of Knowledge (PMBOK® Guide).* 7th ed. PMI.

Rayes, A. and S. Salam. 2022. *Internet of Things From Hype to Reality: The Road to Digitization.* 3rd ed. Cham: Springer.

Rebala, G., A. Ravi, and S. Churiwala. 2019. *An Introduction to Machine Learning.* Cham: Springer.

Recardo, R.J. 2008. *Organization Design: A Practical Methodology and Toolkit.* HRD Press.

Reinhartz-Berger, I., A. Sturm, T. Clark, S. Cohen and J. Bettin, eds. 2013. *Domain Engineering: Product Lines, Languages, and Conceptual Models.* Berlin: Springer-Verlag.

Richardson, G.L. 2019. *Project Management: Theory and Practice.* 3rd ed. Boca Raton: CRC Press.

Rijmenam van, M. 2020. *The Organisation of Tomorrow: How AI, Blockchain and Analytics Turn Your Business Into a Data Organisation.* New York, NY: Routledge

Rissen, P. 2019. *Experiment-Driven Product Development: How to Use a Data-Informed Approach to Learn, Iterate, and Succeed Faster.* Delaware: Apress.

Roberts, T. and S.J. Tonna. 2022. *Risk Modeling: Practical Applications of Artificial Intelligence, Machine Learning, and Deep Learning.* Hoboken: Wiley.

Robson, K. 2013. *Service-Ability: Create a Customer Centric Culture and Achieve Competitive Advantage.* Hoboken: Wiley.

Roser, C. 2017. *Faster, Better, Cheaper in the History of Manufacturing: From the Stone Age to Lean Manufacturing and Beyond.* Boca Raton: CRC Press.

Roy, D.B. and W. Zeng. 2015. *Social Multimedia Signals: A Signal Processing Approach to Social Network Phenomena.* Cham: Springer.

Royer, D. 2013. *Enterprise Identity Management: Investment Decision Support Approach.* Berlin: Springer-Verlag.

Rust, R.T. and M. Huang. 2021. *The Feeling Economy: How Artificial Intelligence Is Creating an Era of Empathy.* Cham: Palgrave Macmillan.

Sanders, W.C. 2019. *Basic Principles of Nanotechnology.* Boca Raton: CRC Press.

Scannell, J.W., A. Blanckley, H. Boldon, and B. Warrington. 2012. "Diagnosing the Decline in Pharmaceutical R&D Efficiency." *Nature Reviews Drug Discovery* 11, pp. 191–200.

Schaeffer, E. and D. Sovie. 2019. *Reinventing the Product: How to Transform Your Business and Create Value in the Digital Age.* London: Kogan Page.

Schmidlin, N. 2014. *The Art of Company Valuation and Financial Statement Analysis: A Value Investors Guide With Real-life Case Studies.* West Sussex: Wiley.

Schuhmacher, A., O. Gassmann, and M. Hinder. 2016. "Changing R&D Models in Research-Based Pharmaceutical Companies." *Journal of Translational Medicine* 14, pp. 105–115.

Senge, P.M. 1990. *The Fifth Discipline: The Art and Practice of the Learning Organization*. London: Random House.

Shehory, O. and A. Sturm. 2014. *Agent-Oriented Software Engineering: Reflections on Architectures, Methodologies, Languages, and Frameworks*. Berlin: Springer-Verlag.

Shukla, U. 2020. "Privacy and Security Challenges Based on IoT Architecture." In *IoT Security and Privacy Program*, eds. S. Pal, V.G. Diaz, and D. Le. Boca Raton: CRC Press.

Shull, F., J. Singer, and D.I.K. Sjoberg, eds. 2008. *Guide to Advanced Empirical Software Engineering*. London: Springer-Verlag.

Sisney, L. 2021. *Designed to Scale: How to Structure Your Business for Exponential Growth*. Organizational Physics Inc.

Smith, A.C.T., F. Sutherland, and D.H. Gilbert. 2017. *Reinventing Innovation-Designing the Dual Organization*. Cham: Palgrave Macmillan.

Smith, B.E. 2014. *Green Computing: Tools and Techniques for Saving Energy, Money and Resources*. Boca Raton: CRC Press.

Stackowiak, R. and T. Kelly. 2020. *Design Thinking in Software and AI Projects: Proving Ideas Through Rapid Prototyping*. Delaware: Apress.

Stark, J. 2015. *Product Lifecycle Management*. 3rd ed. *Cham: Springer*.

Stark, R. 2022. *Virtual Product Creation in Industry: The Difficult Transformation From IT Enabler Technology to Core Engineering Concepts*. Berlin: Springer-Verlag.

Steiber, A. 2014. *The Google Model: Managing Continuous Innovation in a Rapidly Changing World*. Cham: Springer.

Steiber, A. and S. Alange. 2016. *The Silicon Valley Model: Management for Entrepreneurship*. Cham: Springer.

Steinicke, F. 2016. *Being Really Virtual: Immersive Natives and the Future of Virtual Reality*. Cham: Springer.

Suwelack, T., M. Stegemann, and F.X. Ang. 2022. *Creating a Customer Experience-Centric Startup: A Step-by-Step Framework*. Cham: Springer.

Sztipanovits, J., S. Ying, I. Cohen, D. Corman, J. Davis, H. Khurana, P. Mosterman, V. Prasad, and L. Stormo. 2012. *Strategic R&D Opportunities for 21st Century Cyber-Physical Systems*. Technical report, Steering Committee for Foundation in Innovation for Cyber-Physical Systems.

Tanwar, S. 2022. *Blockchain Technology: From Theory to Practice*. Singapore: Springer.

Tarasova, A.V. and Y.V. Vertakova. 2022. "Methodology for Assessing Intellectual Capital of a Business." In *Imitation Modeling as a Scientific and Methodological*

*Approach to Studying the Digital Economy Markets*, eds. E.G. Popkova. Cham: Springer.

Tigelaar, H. 2020. *How Transistor Area Shrank by 1 Million Fold*. Cham: Springer.

Toylan, N. V. and K. Çakırel. 2020. "Structure and Strategy in Virtual Organizations: Strategies for Virtual Travel Organizations." In *Digital Business Strategies in Blockchain Ecosystems: Transformational Design and Future of Global Business*, eds. U. Hacioglu. Cham: Springer.

Tseng, M.M. and F.T. Piller. 2003. *The Customer Centric Enterprise: Advances in Mass Customization and Personalization*. Berlin: Springer-Verlag.

Tsigkas, A.C. 2013. *The Lean Enterprise: From the Mass Economy to the Economy of One*. Berlin: Springer-Verlag.

Veldsman, T.H. 2019. *Designing Fit-for-Purpose Organizations: A Comprehensive, Integrated Route Map*. Randburg: KR Publishing.

Venanzi, D. 2012. *Financial Performance Measures and Value Creation: The State of the Art*. Milan: Springer.

Verma, J.K. and S. Paul, eds. 2022. *Advances in Augmented Reality and Virtual Reality*. Singapore: Springer.

Voigt, K.I., O. Buliga, and K. Michl. 2017. *Business Model Pioneers: How Innovators Successfully Implement New Business Models*. Cham: Springer.

Vuppalapati, R. 2021. *Democratization of Artificial Intelligence for the Future of Humanity*. Boca Raton: CRC Press.

Waterman, R.H., T.J. Peters, and J.R. Phillips. 1980. "Structure Is Not Organization." *Business Horizons* 23, no. 3, pp. 14–26.

Wellman, J.L. 2009. *Organizational Learning: How Companies and Institutions Manage and Apply Knowledge*. New York, NY: Palgrave Macmillan.

Wells, P., ed. 2019. *Contemporary Operations and Logistics: Achieving Excellence in Turbulent*. Cham: Palgrave Macmillan.

Whitehead, J. and M. Peckham. 2022. *Network Leadership: Navigating and Shaping Our Interconnected World*. New York, NY: Routledge.

Wieringa, R.J. 2014. *Design Science Methodology: For Information Systems and Software Engineering*. Cham: Springer.

Wilson, G. 2020. *DevSecOps: A Leader's Guide to Producing Secure Software Without Compromising Flow, Feedback and Continuous Improvement*.

Yovanno, D.A. 2022. *The Partner Economy: How Modern Businesses Find New Customers, Grow Revenue and Deliver Exceptional Experiences*. Hoboken: Wiley.

Yu, C.H.A. 2022. *Data Mining and Exploration: From Traditional Statistics to Modern Data Science*. New York, NY: Boca Raton: CRC Press.

# About the Author

**Vivek Kale** has more than two decades of professional IT experience, during which he has worked with consulting organizations like TCS, Tata Unisys (now merged with TCS), i-flex solutions (now merged with Oracle Corp.), Syntel US, and a couple of startup businesses. He has handled and consulted on various aspects of enterprisewide information modeling, enterprise architectures, business process redesign, and e-business architectures.

He also has industrial experience having worked as Group CIO of Essar Group (now ArcelorMittal Nippon Steel (AM/NS India), the steel/oil and gas major of India, as well as Raymond Ltd., the textile and apparel major of India. He is a seasoned practitioner in enhancing business agility through digital transformation of business models, enterprise architecture, and business processes, enabling the process-oriented enterprise and enhancing IT-enabled enterprise intelligence (EQ).

He is the author of books on cloud and big data computing. He is author of *Inverting the Paradox of Excellence: How Companies Use Variations for Business Excellence and How Enterprise Variations Are Enabled by SAP* (CRC Press 2014) and *Agile Network Businesses* (CRC Press 2017). He is also the author of *Digital Transformation of Enterprise Architecture* (CRC Press 2019).

## Books by Vivek Kale *(additional details on each of the books are available on amazon.com)*

Parallel Computing Architectures and APIs: IoT Big Data Stream Processing (CRC Press 2020)

Digital Transformation of Enterprise Architecture (CRC Press 2019)

Enterprise Process Management Systems: Engineering Process-centric Enterprise Systems using BPMN 2.0 (CRC Press 2018)

Creating Smart Enterprises: Leveraging Cloud, Big Data, Web, Social Media, Mobile and IoT Technologies (CRC Press 2018)

Enterprise Performance Intelligence and Decision Patterns (CRC Press 2018)

Agile Network Businesses: Collaboration, Coordination, and Competitive Advantage (CRC Press 2017)

Big Data Computing: A Guide for Business and Technology Managers (CRC Press 2017)

Enhancing Enterprise Intelligence: Leveraging ERP, CRM, SCM, PLM, BPM, and BI (CRC Press 2016)

Guide to Cloud Computing for Business and Technology Managers: From Distributed Computing to Cloudware Applications (CRC Press 2015)

Inverting the Paradox of Excellence: How Companies Use Variations for Business Excellence and How Enterprise Variations Are Enabled by SAP (CRC Press 2015)

Implementing SAP CRM: The Guide for Business and Technology Managers (CRC Press 2015)

Implementing Oracle Siebel CRM (Tata McGraw-Hill 2010)

Implementing SAP R/3: A Guide for Business and Technology Managers (Sams 2000)

# Index

Note: Page numbers followed by f and t refers to figures and tables respectively.

## OTHER TITLES IN THE ENTREPRENEURSHIP AND SMALL BUSINESS MANAGEMENT COLLECTION

Scott Shane, Case Western University, Editor

- *The Most Common Entrepreneurial Mistakes and How to Avoid Them* by Lisa J Peck-MacDonald
- *The Hybrid Entrepreneur* by Kevin J. Scanlon
- *Stuck Entrepreneurs* by Jay J. Silverberg
- *Teaching Old Dogs New Tricks* by Thomas Waters
- *Building Business Capacity* by Sheryl Hardin
- *The Entrepreneurial Adventure* by Oliver James
- *So, You Bought a Franchise. Now What?* by David Roemer
- *The Startup Masterplan* by Nikhil Agarwal and Krishiv Agarwal
- *Managing Health and Safety in a Small Business* by Jacqueline Jeynes
- *Modern Devil's Advocacy* by Robert Koshinskie
- *Dead Fish Don't Swim Upstream* by Jay J. Silverberg and Bruce E. McLean
- *Founders, Freelancers & Rebels* by Helen Jane Campbell
- *The 8 Superpowers of Successful Entrepreneurs* by Marina Nicholas
- *Navigating the New Normal* by Rodd Mann
- *Time Management for Unicorns* by Giulio D'Agostino

## Concise and Applied Business Books

The Collection listed above is one of 30 business subject collections that Business Expert Press has grown to make BEP a premiere publisher of print and digital books. Our concise and applied books are for…

- Professionals and Practitioners
- Faculty who adopt our books for courses
- Librarians who know that BEP's Digital Libraries are a unique way to offer students ebooks to download, not restricted with any digital rights management
- Executive Training Course Leaders
- Business Seminar Organizers

Business Expert Press books are for anyone who needs to dig deeper on business ideas, goals, and solutions to everyday problems. Whether one print book, one ebook, or buying a digital library of 110 ebooks, we remain the affordable and smart way to be business smart. For more information, please visit www.businessexpertpress.com, or contact sales@businessexpertpress.com.

www.ingramcontent.com/pod-product-compliance
Lightning Source LLC
Chambersburg PA
CBHW061151220326
41599CB00025B/4449